1 GOOD THINGS 2 WITH 3 MARTHA 4 STEWART 5 LIVING 6

simple home

solutions

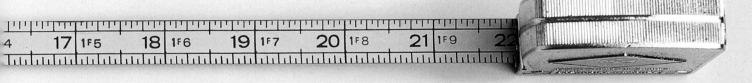

FROM THE EDITORS OF MARTHA STEWART LIVING

CLARKSON/POTTER PUBLISHERS
NEW YORK

Originally published in book form by
Martha Stewart Living Omnimedia, Inc.,
in 2004. Published simultaneously by
Clarkson Potter/Publishers, Oxmoor
House, Inc., and Leisure Arts.

A portion of this work was previously published in MARTHA STEWART LIVING.

Published by Clarkson Potter/
Publishers, New York, New York.
Member of the Crown Publishing
Group, a division of Random House,
Inc.; www.clarksonpotter.com.
CLARKSON N. POTTER is a trade-
mark and POTTER and colophon
are registered trademarks of
Random House, Inc.

Printed in the United States of America.

Library of Congress Cataloging-in-
Publication Data: Simple home solu-
tions/by the editors of Martha Stewart
Living.—1st ed. Includes index.
1. Home economics. I. Martha Stewart living. TX145.S58 2004
640—dc22   2003027379

ISBN 1-4000-5485-0
10 9 8 7 6 5 4 3 2 1 First Edition

CONTENTS

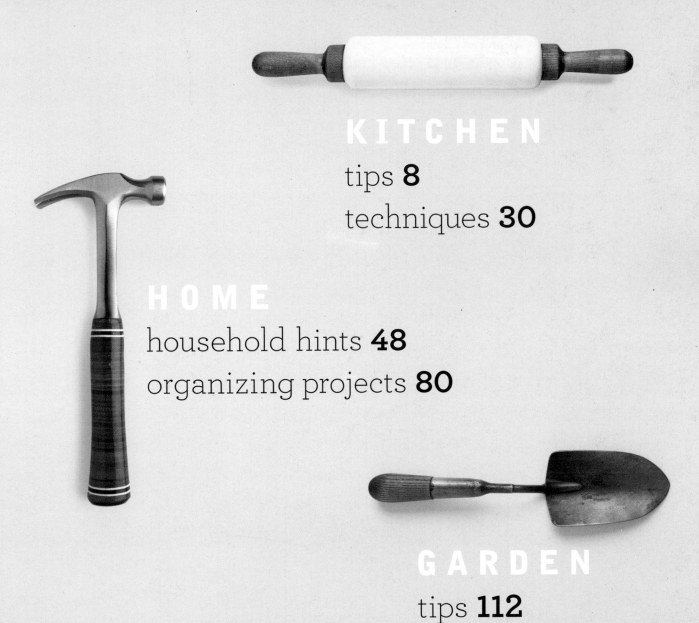

Sharing clever solutions to common household problems has a long tradition. For centuries, tips and secrets have been passed down from one generation to the next. In fact, most of us draw on wisdom of this type all the time—usually without realizing it. We place a box of baking soda in the refrigerator to absorb odors, or drop a slice of apple into a bag of hardened brown sugar to soften it, rarely giving thought to how we came to learn these things in the first place. The simple home solutions in this book provide the same sort of insight. We offer strategies for dealing with common dilemmas—a stubborn jar lid that just won't

budge, for example, a pulled hem on a pant leg, or a terra-cotta planter covered with fungus. We've gathered our favorite Good Things—instantly recognizable for their simplicity, practicality, and economy—from MARTHA STEWART LIVING to create a book filled with ideas and projects you'll be eager to incorporate into your regular routine.

Within each chapter—Kitchen, Home, and Garden—you'll discover new ways to make better use of time, energy, and space—and in some cases, all of the above. In the kitchen, we teach you the quickest ways to accomplish small jobs, as well as things you can do ahead to save time as you cook. The home chapter is made up of maintenance and repair information, home-improvement hints, and clothing-care

advice, including an invaluable stain-removal chart for fabrics. We have also included more than forty organizing projects that will bring order to your home. The tips in the garden chapter emphasize the most effective ways to propagate, nurture, and display plants in the house and garden, as well as how to organize and care for containers and equipment.

Each chapter ends with a glossary of tools—some of which are used for the projects in this book, others we think are simply worth getting to know better. These glossaries are not intended to be comprehensive; rather, they are designed to demystify uncommon equipment, such as grommet kits and dandelion spikes, and to suggest what to look for in everyday implements like hammers and wire whisks.

Whether you're looking to solve a particular problem or to take measures to prevent one, *Simple Home Solutions* is a reference guide you're sure to reach for time and time again. Think of it as household wisdom you can store on a bookshelf.

RIPENING PEACHES
To ripen peaches quickly, place them in a paper bag and keep it closed for two or three days. Ethylene gas is concentrated this way, speeding up the ripening process naturally. To slow the ripening, leave the bag open, or place it in the refrigerator.

KITCHEN

Ask any cook—your grandmother, your best friend, or a professional chef—to share a favorite tip for saving time or money in the kitchen, and you'll likely get an immediate answer. Wonder aloud at how best to perform a kitchen task and advice will surely follow. There's a reason for the enthusiastic response such a question generates, and it has more to do with the pleasure of sharing than simply conveying information. Learning a better way to stuff a chicken will save you time and effort, and may even elicit exclamations of surprise. There are many such hints in this two-part chapter: tips for making kitchen tasks more efficient, and techniques to help you cook like a pro. Try them out in your own kitchen. Then do what countless others have done before you: Pass along what you've learned, with pleasure.

It is always so much fun—as well as immensely satisfying— to discover a new or innovative way to do a task that is easier, simpler, or even just a bit less time-consuming. –Martha

HOT POTATOES The best way to keep mashed potatoes warm without ruining their fluffy texture is to place them in a heatproof bowl set over a pan of simmering water. Loosely covered with a lid or foil, they can be kept warm for up to two hours. (This is also a good way to re-heat them.) Warming the serving bowl can also help the potatoes arrive at the table steaming hot. Just run the bowl (preferably heavy ceramic or stainless steel) under hot tap water for a few minutes. Dry completely, then fill with the potatoes. These techniques can also be used for other puréed vegetables, such as winter squash and turnips.

LESS-MESS TOMATOES

Chopping quantities of canned tomatoes for use in soups and sauces is a messy task. Rather than removing the tomatoes and slicing, use a pair of kitchen shears to cut them while they're still in the tin. Not only does this prevent spatters—you'll also have one less bowl to wash.

SIEVE SPLATTER GUARD A splatter guard keeps grease spots on your stove to a minimum when frying, and helps protect the cook as well. If you don't have one, a large sieve can stand in. Place it facedown over the food cooking in the pan. For safety, turn both handles toward the back of the stove, resting the sieve's handle on top of the pan's.

SAVING TOMATO PASTE

Keep tomato paste from going to waste when your recipe calls for just a tablespoon or two. Open both ends of the can; discard one end, and keep the other in place. Wrap the can in plastic wrap; freeze overnight. Use the metal end to push the frozen paste out of the open end; discard can. Tightly wrap unused portion, and store in the freezer for up to three months, slicing off what you need as you cook.

CALCULATING MOLD CAPACITY You are more likely to use a fluted mold when you know exactly how many cups it holds. Simply fill irregularly shaped molds with water, and then pour the water into a liquid measuring cup. Write the cup measurement on an index card and store it with the mold for future reference.

OPENING JARS Stubborn jar lids can wreak havoc on wrists and fingers. Instead of wrestling with a lid, place one rubber band around the jar and another around the lid. Twisting the lid while gripping both bands should create enough friction to open the jar. It also helps to hit the bottom of the jar several times with the heel of your hand.

HEATING A TEAPOT Prevent a chilly ceramic, china, or porcelain teapot from drawing the warmth from your tea before you've had your second cup. To keep tea from cooling too quickly, first fill the pot with very hot water (either from the tap or boiled on the stove), then pour it out before you start steeping the tea.

ENVELOPE FUNNEL Transferring dried grains, beans, and other dry goods from bags to airtight jars keeps them fresh, but the process can cause them to spill all over the countertop. If you don't have a funnel, use an envelope instead. Cut off a corner so you have a triangle, snip off the closed point, and open it into a cone.

soup tip Toss the rind of a hard cheese such as Parmesan into a simmering soup or stock—as Italian cooks do—to thicken it and impart a rich flavor. Freeze leftover rinds, then pull one out whenever you're making soup; remove rind from soup before serving.

A HINT OF GARLIC
Sliced or minced garlic often chars when cooked too quickly over high heat, and its flavor may prove to be too strong. To lend a mild garlic flavor to stir-fries, such as sautéed greens, spear a large peeled clove with a fork and use it to stir as you cook. When you move the ingredients around in the pan, the greens will be infused with a gentle garlic flavor and aroma.

HERB CORN BASTER

A bundle of herbs makes a handy basting brush, perfect for corn on the cob. The brush gives the butter—and the corn—flavor. Select a combination of herbs, such as thyme, oregano, parsley, rosemary, and marjoram. Bunch them together, and bind the stems with a length of twine or several rubber bands. Dip the bundle in melted butter, and brush over the kernels.

MORE COLORFUL BROTH

A soup may taste delicious, but if it looks deep and rich in color, it's even more appealing. To give a broth or soup base a deeper, more amber hue, leave the skin on the onions after you've cut them into halves or quarters. The skins will beautifully color the stock; strain before using it as broth or in a soup.

SLICING GOAT CHEESE
A knife isn't the best tool for cutting goat cheese into neat portions. For better results, lay a length of unflavored dental floss or fine thread beneath the log of cheese, cross the ends over the top (but don't knot), and then pull the thread taut. The cheese rounds should fall away.

ROASTED GARLIC SPREAD
For a simple—and flavorful—appetizer, try this no-mince method for making garlic bread. Split a head of garlic in half crosswise and drizzle with olive oil. Roast, wrapped in aluminum foil, in a 375 degree oven for about forty-five minutes. The softened cloves will spread easily on toasted bread.

KEEPING CHOPPED GARLIC
Mincing garlic is time-consuming, so if you need a large amount for a recipe, complete the task in advance. Peel several heads of garlic, mince them in a food processor, and refrigerate, covered with olive oil, in an airtight jar. When you are ready to cook, just open the refrigerator, and spoon some out of the jar. For safety reasons, do not store the chopped garlic for more than one week.

POWDERED MUSHROOMS To add an earthy flavor to breadcrumbs or cracker mixes, keep a jar of ground mushrooms in your spice drawer. They're easy to make—just pulverize assorted dried wild mushrooms, such as porcini and morels, with a mortar and pestle or in a spice grinder. The powder also works well as a meat rub, or sprinkled over roasted vegetables.

HOW LONG WILL MEAT, POULTRY, OR FISH KEEP?

food	refrigerator (34 to 40 degrees)	freezer (at or below 0 degrees)
RAW CHICKEN OR TURKEY	1 or 2 days	6 to 12 months
RAW BEEF ROASTS OR STEAKS	3 to 5 days	6 to 12 months
RAW LAMB ROASTS OR CHOPS	3 to 5 days	6 to 9 months
LEFTOVER COOKED CHICKEN OR TURKEY	3 or 4 days	4 to 6 months
LEFTOVER COOKED MEAT	3 or 4 days	2 or 3 months
LEFTOVER COOKED FISH	3 or 4 days	3 months

WHAT TEMPERATURE SHOULD IT REACH?

For food-safety reasons, it is best to cook your food to these temperatures:

ground beef, veal, lamb, or pork
160 DEGREES

beef, veal, or lamb roasts, steaks, or chops
145 TO 170 DEGREES

pork roasts, steaks, or chops
160 TO 170 DEGREES

ground chicken or turkey
165 DEGREES

whole chicken or turkey
180 DEGREES

NEATER MEAT CARVING

If your carving board doesn't have a well to catch juices, set it in a rimmed baking sheet before you begin to slice. Not only will you be able to collect the juices for sauces and gravies, but you won't have to wipe drips or spills from the countertop afterward.

cracker tip

When humidity leaves you with a box of damp, soggy crackers, restore their crisp-ness by placing them in a 225 degree oven for up to five min-utes, depending on the type of cracker. Keep checking every minute or so, until crackers are dry.

BREADING MIXES There isn't always day-old bread around when you need crumbs to coat chicken cutlets or fish fillets. When you do have stale bread, make a few sea-soned blends and freeze them in resealable plastic bags for up to one month. Remove crust, cut bread into cubes, and then pulse cubes in the food processor until fine or coarse crumbs form. One 8-ounce loaf will yield about 2¼ cups breadcrumbs, which you can use as the base for any of the following mixtures. FOR LEMON-SAGE BREADCRUMBS, add 3 tablespoons finely grated lemon zest and 5 tablespoons finely chopped fresh sage. FOR COCONUT-LIME BREADCRUMBS, add ½ cup toasted, unsweetened shredded coconut, 2½ tablespoons finely grated lime zest, and ¾ teaspoon cayenne pepper. FOR ALMOND AND GARAM MASALA BREADCRUMBS, add ½ cup chopped and toasted sliced almonds and 2 teaspoons garam masala. FOR PARMESAN-OREGANO BREAD-CRUMBS, add 3½ tablespoons chopped fresh oregano (or 1 teaspoon dried) and ¾ cup finely grated Parmesan cheese. Season breadcrumb mixtures with coarse salt and freshly ground black pepper. Just before cooking, dredge chicken or fish in flour, then in beaten egg, and finally in the seasoned breadcrumbs.

STORING WATERCRESS

Watercress is at its best when tender and bright green. To keep it from wilting, stand the greens in a glass of ice water, cover with a plastic bag, and refrigerate. Refill the water as necessary. The watercress should stay fresh for several days. This method works well for parsley, too.

BRIGHT PESTO Fresh pesto turns from emerald green to a dull brown if exposed to air for too long. While the flavor of the sauce is not affected, it looks less appetizing. To prevent discoloration, create a barrier by pouring a thin layer of olive oil over the top of the pesto, then keep it refrigerated in an airtight container.

SAVING EGGS After separating eggs for a recipe that calls for only whites or yolks, pour the remaining egg parts into an airtight container, and freeze. To prevent the yolks from gelling, add a pinch of salt (for use in main dishes) or a heaping teaspoon of sugar (for desserts) for every four yolks. The day before using, transfer the container to the refrigerator, and let the egg parts thaw overnight.

PROTECTING GRAINS To discourage pests from setting up home in your grains and legumes, try this trick: Transfer the dry goods from their plastic bags into airtight jars, then drop a dried chile pepper or two or a large bay leaf into the jar. The chile's oils and the fragrance of the bay leaf act as natural repellents.

INSTANT BREAKFAST

You can relax in the morning and still have homemade goods for breakfast. Fill resealable plastic bags with the dry ingredients for favorite pancake or muffin recipes. Using a permanent marker, write the recipe's wet ingredients, along with cooking instructions, on the bags. Store in the freezer for up to one month.

ICE CREAM SAVER

To prevent condensation from forming an icy crust on your ice cream, press a small piece of waxed paper against its surface before you place the lid back on the container. Do this each time you indulge, and every scoop will taste as creamy as the first.

PERFECT EGG WHITES

Just a speck of yolk can make egg whites impossible to whip, and wear out even the most determined cook's arm. To remove small bits of yolk, use the egg-shell as a scoop. The yolk will be attracted back into the shell, and a jagged edge will capture even the tiniest spot of yellow.

CLARIFYING BUTTER There's a quicker way to clarify (remove the solids from) melted butter than the traditional twenty-minute stovetop method. Place the butter in a deep glass container, and micro-wave for two minutes. Skim off any floating solids, then pour the clear yellow liquid into a cup until you reach the solids at the bottom. One stick of butter (½ cup) should yield ⅓ cup clarified butter.

BUTTERING BAKING PANS

A pastry brush lets you coat any baking pan, even deep muffin tins and madeleine molds, with softened butter. It also ensures that all hard-to-reach nooks get covered. To make unmolding and cleanup easier, coat the areas between the pan's cups as well.

TESTING CARAMEL

Recipes for caramel call for the syrup to reach a specific shade of amber—light, medium, or dark—before proceeding to the next step. To test the color, use strips of parchment or white card stock. Dip a new strip into the caramel every few seconds until you see the right shade.

DUSTING WITH COCOA

In theory, chocolate cake is so appealing it can be served to guests with nothing more than a dusting of confectioners' sugar. The problem is, white flour used to coat the pan often shows. Instead, try dusting the pan with cocoa powder. It does the same job with invisible results.

BETTER FRUITCAKES AND MUFFINS To keep nuts, dried fruits, berries, or chocolate chips from sinking to the bottom of a batter, toss them in a tablespoon or two of flour set aside from the recipe's dry ingredients. Don't increase the amount of flour, as this may cause the recipe to fail by upsetting the balance of ingredients.

BAKER'S SACHET

Dried beans make perfect pie weights, which help an unfilled crust maintain its shape as it bakes. A layer of cheesecloth keeps them neat and at the ready. For a standard-size pie plate, take one pound of dry beans and wrap them loosely enough that the beans are able to spread out and cover the bottom of the pan. Cinch the bundle with kitchen twine. After each use, let the pouch cool, and then store it in an airtight container. Discard the bundle if the beans develop a musty odor, or after about ten uses.

BAKING SUBSTITUTIONS	
instead of 1 cup...	you can use
SELF-RISING FLOUR	1 cup all-purpose flour plus 1½ teaspoons baking powder and ⅛ teaspoon salt
CAKE FLOUR	1 cup minus 2 tablespoons all-purpose flour
LIGHT-BROWN SUGAR	1 cup white sugar plus 1 tablespoon molasses
MOLASSES	¾ cup dark-brown sugar plus ¼ cup water
WHOLE-WHEAT FLOUR	1 cup minus 2 tablespoons all-purpose flour plus 2 tablespoons wheat germ

EASY STUFFING Rather than grapple with a whole raw chicken on the kitchen counter, where it's awkwardly positioned for stuffing and could contaminate your preparation area, place it in a high-sided bowl. Arrange chicken with the cavity opening facing up for easy access.

MESS-FREE PREP BOARD When chicken needs nothing but a little seasoning, there's no reason to make a mess of your work surface. Lay down a sheet of plastic wrap first. As long as you do not do any cutting, the plastic serves as a barrier against bacteria. When you're finished, carefully fold up the plastic and throw it away.

citrus zest tip After you've squeezed all of the juice from a lemon or lime, freeze the spent halves in a resealable plastic bag (for up to three months). Grate the desired amount of frozen peel the next time you are using a recipe that calls for fresh zest.

BOWL HOLDER Whipping up a vinaigrette can make you wish you had three hands—one to whisk, one to pour the oil, and one to hold the bowl steady. A damp kitchen towel can make things easier. Just twist the towel securely around the base of the bowl to hold it in place.

JUICIER LEMONS
To get the most juice from a lemon, roll it firmly between your palm and the counter before cutting and squeezing. The pressure created as you roll crushes the fruit's inner membranes, releasing more juice.

CLEANING BEET-STAINED HANDS As anyone who has cooked with beets knows, their juice leaves persistent stains on the hands. (It's no wonder that beets have long been used as a fabric dye.) To remove the color, rub your hands with a sliced raw potato under running water. This trick works for turmeric stains, too.

QUICK BLENDER CLEANUP Blenders are easiest to wash if they're not left standing too long after use. To loosen residue, fill the jar right away with ½ cup water and ½ cup baking soda, then run blender briefly. Empty jar, disassemble, and wash all pieces with warm soap and water. Your blender will shine in no time.

CUTTING BOARD CARE
Wooden cutting boards require special maintenance if they are to last and stay free of food-borne bacteria. Every few weeks, sprinkle a generous portion of coarse salt over the board's surface, and rub it with the cut side of a lemon half. Rinse well with hot water, and dry completely.

clean cookbook tip To protect a cookbook from splatters while you cook, slip it into a gallon-size resealable plastic bag. This trick also keeps the book open to the recipe you are using.

COOKBOOK HELPERS Make a cookbook even more useful by adding a bookmark, a pencil holder, and a pocket to collect notes and clipped recipes. For the pencil holder, use white craft glue to attach a piece of wide grosgrain ribbon horizontally across the middle of the book's inside back cover. Then place a pencil on top of the ribbon and glue the ribbon back onto itself, creating a loop. For the bookmark, glue a portion of a narrow ribbon along the spine edge of the inside back cover, leaving enough hanging free to tuck between two pages and dangle out the bottom. To make the pocket, glue an envelope, slightly smaller than the back endpaper, over both ribbons.

How exciting it is to learn something new—a technique for peeling kiwis or creating a lattice top for your favorite pie. Here are some wonderful, clever ways to do things differently than you have before, which will make you smile and, better yet, make you more facile in the kitchen. –Martha

NO-STICK GARLIC

There's a foolproof way to mince garlic quickly, without having it stick to your knife. Sprinkle coarse salt and a drop of olive oil over the cloves before you chop. The salt crystals act as an abrasive, helping to pulverize the cloves, while the slickness of the olive oil allows the garlic to slide easily off the blade. To make a paste, lay the side of your knife on top of the chopped garlic, and drag it over the top several times, applying even pressure.

CHEESE SHAVINGS

Thin curls of Parmesan make an elegant addition to pastas, soups, and salads. But creating fine slices with a knife is challenging, and a grater doesn't yield pieces of the right size or shape. A vegetable peeler works better. Rub a drop of olive oil over the blades for best results.

PEELING PEARL ONIONS Rather than trying to remove the dry, papery skins from a bunch of pearl onions one at a time, place them in a bowl and cover with boiling water. Let the onions sit for a few minutes, then cut off the root ends with a sharp knife. The flavorful pearls will pop right out of their softened skins.

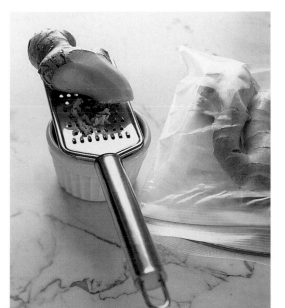

EASY-TO-GRATE GINGER

Fresh ginger has fibers that can separate from the root's juicy flesh when it's grated. But if you freeze the whole unpeeled root first, it will grate neatly. Remove ginger from the freezer, peel and grate the part you need while it's still frozen, and return the remainder to the freezer. Wrapped tightly in plastic, it will last for several months.

QUICK-PEEL TOMATOES

Though other techniques for skinning tomatoes exist, the fastest method is this: Score a small X in the bottom of each tomato with a paring knife. Bring a large pot of water to a boil; meanwhile, prepare an ice bath. Lower three or four tomatoes at a time into the boiling water for about ten seconds. With a slotted spoon, transfer the blanched tomatoes to the ice bath. When cool enough to handle, about thirty seconds, remove the tomatoes and pull off the skins with your fingers or a small knife. See below to learn how to create a seasoning with the skins.

TOMATO POWDER

Add a burst of flavor and color to pastas, salads, or deviled eggs. Preheat oven to 225 degrees. Spread tomato skins on a rimmed baking sheet lined with lightly oiled parchment paper. Bake until deep red and papery, about forty-five minutes, rotating sheet halfway through. Grind peels to a powder in a spice mill or clean coffee grinder. Store in an airtight container at room temperature for up to one month.

DRYING PEPPERS The best way to preserve an abundance of colorful chile peppers is to hang them in a sunny window for several weeks. To string the peppers, knot a length of kitchen twine around the stems, beginning at one end and working your way up. Tie a loop at the loose end of the twine, and hang from a small hook.

SKINNING SWEET POTATOES Boiling unpeeled sweet potatoes preserves their nutritional value, but removing the skins after cooking can be tedious. Place the cooked potatoes in an ice-water bath for a minute or two; when the skins pucker, cup a potato in your hands, and use your thumbs to split the skin, releasing the flesh.

EASY BLANCHING Don't let crunchy green vegetables, such as sugar snap peas, end up overcooked and mushy. After briefly boiling then draining the vegetables, dunk them, still in the colander, in a large bowl of ice water. After about one minute, lift the colander from the bowl; the vegetables will be crisp, bright, and ready to eat.

broccoli technique Broccoli stems are tougher and woodier than the florets, but both will cook in the same amount of time if you first slit a deep X in the stems with a paring knife.

QUICK CORN Cooking fresh corn usually involves waiting for a big pot of water to boil and then dropping the cobs in, hoping they'll all fit. Instead, bring just two inches of water to a boil in a stockpot, then stand cobs with stem sides down in the pot or in its pasta insert. Cover and steam until corn changes color, six to eight minutes.

STEAMING ARTICHOKES Instead of buying a special artichoke steamer, improvise with coffee mugs. First, trim the leaves with kitchen shears, then rub the clipped ends with a cut lemon to prevent darkening. Place each artichoke, stem up, in a mug; set mugs in a pot with an inch of simmering water. Cover; steam for one hour.

GRILLING CHICKENS

Barbecuing whole chickens on a charcoal grill can frustrate the outdoor chef, since the birds tend to char before cooking all the way through. The solution is to create an indirect heat source. After lighting the coals, push them against the wall of the grill, creating an open area in the center. Squeeze two disposable square foil baking pans (one inside the other) into this space to catch drips and prevent flare-ups. Watch the chickens carefully, changing their positions so they cook evenly. If necessary, cover the grill intermittently to quell the flames.

STEADYING KABOBS

Have you ever tried to flip a kabob on the grill only to discover that it was the skewer—not the fish, meat, or vegetables—that turned over? If you use two skewers, one will balance the other, creating a makeshift rack. The extra handle also decreases the likelihood that food will break free and drop through the grates of the grill.

IMPROMPTU FISH STEAMER If a recipe calls for a fish steamer and you don't have one, assemble your own from common kitchenware. Fill a rimmed baking sheet or roasting pan halfway with water; add a splash of white wine, a few lemon slices, and some herbs, such as thyme sprigs or bay leaves. Place fillets on a wire rack set in the pan; cover loosely with parchment paper and then foil. Press down around edges to trap the steam. Place in a 375 degree oven until the fish is cooked through, about three and a half minutes for a ⅓-inch-thick fillet.

STEMMING CHARD

Why labor with a knife to remove stems from Swiss chard—and other tough-stemmed greens—when running your hand down the stem would be sufficient? First, soak the chard in cool water to remove sediment. Then, holding the stem in one hand, grasp both sides of the stem with your other hand and run your fingers from base to tip, pulling off the leaf. Place damp paper towels over the chard as you work to keep it from drying out.

HOLDING A CHEF'S KNIFE

A good tool works best if you know how to use it. Because a chef's knife broadens from tip to base, it allows strong downward pressure with good control while slicing or chopping. Slide your hand up the handle to hold the base of the blade. Curve your index finger along one side of the knife, and press your straightened thumb along the other.

STRIPPING AND CHOPPING FRESH HERBS To avoid bruising leaves and to maximize flavors, make sure you use the technique best suited for each herb. REMOVING PARSLEY OR CILANTRO LEAVES: Instead of picking off each leaf, hold the stems of the herb bunch in one hand and a chef's knife in the other hand (above left); remove the leaves from the stems using a short, downward motion, turning the bunch as necessary. You'll save time, and any small stems overlooked will become undetectable when chopped. Discard whole stems, or reserve them for another use, such as flavoring soups or sauces. STRIPPING SMALL LEAVES FROM WOODY STEMS: For herbs such as thyme, rosemary, and oregano (above center), grasp the tip of the stem with two fingers. With the other hand, run your thumb and index finger along the stem, from top to bottom, against the direction of the leaves. CHOPPING HERBS: To evenly chop a handful of herb leaves (above right), bunch them under your cupped hand on the cutting board, instead of having them spread out on the board. Chop alongside your curved fingers, pulling back your hand and releasing more herbs a little at a time.

CRISPING CUCUMBERS

To make cucumber slices extra crunchy for salads, arrange them in a colander placed inside a bowl. Sprinkle with salt, cover with ice cubes, and refrigerate for an hour. Pat dry, and refrigerate until ready to use. This method works for radishes and celery, too.

CORING PEARS Sometimes the best tool for the job is one that was designed for another purpose. A melon baller, for example, is perfect for coring pears—which you'll need to do if you plan on poaching them whole. First, slice off the bottom end of each pear, just enough so it will sit upright. Then, scoop out the seeds.

CHOPPING CRANBERRIES Not only is it time-consuming to chop berries by hand, but ripe ones can crush easily in the process and lose a fair amount of their juice. Chop them in a food processor instead. First, freeze fresh berries in a plastic bag overnight, then pulse them in the machine until they're the consistency you need.

seeding technique To remove the seeds from a zucchini or egg-plant you plan to fill with stuffing, loosen seeds first by gently pressing on the vegetable as you roll it on a countertop. Slice in half lengthwise, and use a spoon to scrape out the seeds.

QUICK-PEEL KIWI Here's a great way to skin a kiwi: Trim both ends of the fruit, then carefully ease a tablespoon between the flesh and the fuzzy peel. Turn the kiwi, gently pressing the back of the spoon against the peel as you go. The flesh should slide right out in one piece, perfect for cutting into neat, round slices.

SCOOPING OUT SEEDS Try using an ice cream scoop to remove the seeds from a winter squash. The scoop has edges sharp enough to efficiently cut through the pulp and a bowl deep enough to collect most of the seeds in one pass. You'll end up with a squash cavity that is smooth, clean, and ready for baking.

1

2

3

4

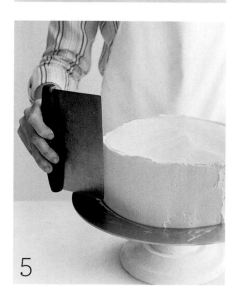

5

6

ICING A LAYER CAKE A few basic steps can help produce a homemade layer cake worthy of a bakery window. We used an 8-inch cake to illustrate.

1. A rotating turntable makes cake decorating easier; if you don't have one, place a plate on an inverted bowl. Place one layer on a cardboard round of the same size; place it on the turntable, securing with a dab of frosting underneath. With a long serrated knife, trim tops off both cake layers to make flat surfaces.

2. Using a small offset spatula, evenly spread the top of the first layer with 1 cup frosting, extending beyond the edges of the cake.

3. Place the other cake layer, cut side down, on top of the frosting; press gently to make it level. With the small spatula, spread 1½ cups more frosting, plus any that is oozing from between the layers, all over the cake, creating a "crumb coat," a thin layer of frosting to seal in crumbs. Refrigerate 15 minutes.

4. Using a large offset spatula, generously coat the chilled cake with 2½ cups frosting, covering the top first. Hold the spatula at a 45 degree angle against the cake and slowly rotate the turntable. If the frosting looks streaky, dip the spatula into hot water, wipe dry, then continue frosting.

5. Hold a bench scraper perpendicular to cake (one edge resting on turntable), and slowly rotate turntable. Touch up any small areas of the cake with the small spatula. Refrigerate 30 minutes.

6. To mark cake for even slicing, fold an 8-inch parchment round in half three times for eight wedges, or four times for sixteen. Unfold, and place on top of the cake. Using fold lines as a guide, lightly mark vertical lines with a bench scraper. Pipe decorations onto cake with additional frosting, if desired.

CHOCOLATE CURLS

To dazzle guests with dessert when you don't have much time, embellish a cake (or cupcakes) with easy-to-make chocolate curls (below). Warm a block of chocolate in your hands, then use a vegetable peeler to create curls (right). The curls will become more graceful as you go, so don't be discouraged by the first few. For longer curls, pour melted chocolate onto a clean, flat surface, spread it to a thin, even thickness, and let it cool. Slowly scrape chocolate up with a bench scraper (far right). Slip a toothpick into the center of the curls when transferring them.

cake removal technique
The next time you bake a cake, let the pan cool for a few minutes on a damp cloth. It should make the difference between a cake that sticks and tears and one that slips out with ease.

  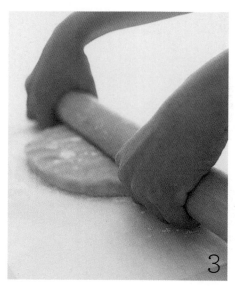

FOOLPROOF PASTRY DOUGH TECHNIQUES 1.CUT IN BUTTER: Using a food processor is the quickest way to incorporate butter, but it's just as easy to do by hand. Cut very cold butter into little pieces, then add them to the dry ingredients. Use two knives or a pastry blender to reduce the lumps to the size of peas. **2.** AVOID CRACKS: Start by patting the dough into the shape called for in your recipe. Then, to preserve the shape and prevent cracks from forming, press down around the edge of the dough with your thumb, making distinct indentations around the perimeter. **3.** ROLL OUT DOUGH: Place your hands on the rolling pin about an inch from either side of the dough's edge. Press down until your knuckles touch the work surface. Start at the center and make indentations all over, until the dough is an even thickness.

EVEN-CRUMB PIECRUST

For a cracker crust of uniform thickness, push crumbs into place with your fingers, then press them down with another pie plate of the same size. For a thinner crust, choose a second plate one size smaller, nestle it on top, and push it gently around the inside of the larger one.

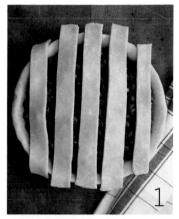

EASY LATTICE PIECRUST An openwork piecrust offers a tempting glimpse of the bubbling fruit within. Working with strips of pastry dough can be intimidating, though, if you haven't done it before. To make the process less daunting, try this technique. Begin by cutting eight strips of dough 1 to 2 inches wide with a pastry wheel or sharp knife. **1.** Lay five strips vertically over the pie. **2.** Fold back the second and fourth strips as shown, and cross the pie at the center with another strip. **3.** Unfold the folded dough strips, then fold back the first, third, and fifth pieces; lay another perpendicular strip halfway between the center strip and the top edge of the pie plate. **4.** Unfold the folded strips, then fold them back from the opposite side. Lay another perpendicular strip halfway between the center strip and the bottom edge. Unfold the last strips; trim any excess. Neatly press ends into outer edges of crust with thumbs.

kitchen-tool glossary A recipe's success depends as much on the tools that are used as on the quality of ingredients. Choose durable equipment, and never place any tool that has joints or removable pieces in the dishwasher. It's worth the investment to buy best-quality kitchen utensils (these will often be stainless steel). You will have to replace them less frequently, and will save money as a result.

SIEVE A sieve with a wide stainless-steel rim (about 1-inch) is best; the mesh should be sturdy so it won't stretch or bend over time. Use it to sift flour or strain soups and sauces.

HAND GRATER This is designed for grating vegetables and hard cheeses, but you can also use it to break up a stick of frozen butter when making pastry dough. Choose a model with large and small holes, plus a straight blade for slicing.

MELON BALLER In addition to its principal use, this gadget is perfect for carving the core from a halved apple or pear, stemming a tomato, or picking the seeds from a watermelon.

WHISK A stainless steel whisk with fine spokes (that wiggle when you shake the handle) is essential. Use it to beat egg whites, smooth sauces and puddings, and "sift" dry ingredients.

KITCHEN SHEARS Look for heavy blades and durable plastic handles. Use shears to butterfly poultry, trim pie dough, cut parchment, snip herbs, remove stems from beans, and slice pizza.

BENCH SCRAPER This is a multi-purpose item, great for cleaning work surfaces and rolling pins, dividing pastry or bread dough into pieces, and transferring diced vegetables to a pan.

ICE CREAM SCOOP Not just for ice cream, a scoop such as this is ideal for measuring equal amounts of cookie dough or muffin batter. For sticky doughs or hard ice cream, dip the tool in water between scoops to help it release more easily. It's a good idea to have scoops in a few different sizes.

MORTAR AND PESTLE The rough, unglazed surfaces of ceramic tools create the friction required for grinding pastes, such as pesto, as well as spice blends from whole seeds and pods.

OFFSET SPATULA This handy tool is used most often for baking—to frost layer cakes, spread batter evenly, lift cookies off baking sheets, or remove brownies from the pan. You can also use it to flip crêpes before serving.

HEATPROOF SPATULA Look for spatulas with silicone heads, which won't melt like rubber ones. Besides stirring hot sauces with it, use it to fold in ingredients or scoop out batter.

VEGETABLE PEELER Generally more comfortable to use than straight ones, U-shaped peelers can shave cheese or chocolate, and make thin ribbons of zucchini, carrots, or asparagus.

CHEF'S KNIFE A high-quality chef's knife is the most essential kitchen tool of all. The knife should have a full tang and forged handle; the blade should be made of high-carbon stainless steel. It is the weight of a chef's knife that does the work, so buy the heaviest one available, and sharpen it regularly—dull knives cause more kitchen accidents than sharp ones. Hone blade with a steel after each use, and sharpen as necessary. Always wash and dry a chef's knife by hand.

WINTER-WEAR CATCHER
Organize scarves, hats, and gloves by placing them inside wire baskets. Label a basket for each family member or clothing type. Start with two 60-inch lengths of 1-by-4 lumber. Place 1½-inch screw hooks at equal intervals down the center of each rail. Suspend rails at a suitable distance from each other using 1½-inch screw eyes on rail ends and 2-inch screw hooks on the bottom of a wooden coat rack.

HOME

If you know exactly what to do when a little mishap occurs (a china pitcher breaks or a button pops off your coat), you can usually remedy the situation in a hurry. But these everyday incidents catch most of us off guard, and as a result we postpone taking care of them. The same is true when it comes to organizing our belongings. Each time a stack of sweaters topples over, we are determined to correct the problem but we don't know exactly how. In this chapter, you'll find clever ways to organize your home, and helpful tips for maintaining it once and for all. Use a pot-lid rack to sort your mail, or eliminate humidity by hanging a bundle of chalk in a closet. Home is for relaxing. Quick projects and easy ideas like these will give you more time for just that.

Here are lots of things that your mother forgot to teach you—or if she did, that you may have forgotten. Refresh your memory, and make your everyday existence just a bit more pleasant, knowing that you have discovered the best way to remove stubborn stains and a better way to hammer a nail into the wall. –Martha

REPLACEMENT BUTTONS

To avoid misplacing the extra buttons that sometimes accompany a new coat or jacket, sew them onto the garment's inside hem. When a button goes missing, you'll have a replacement close at hand.

SWEATER-PILL LIFTER
Many sweater-pill removers contain razor blades—a little unnerving when the sweater in question is your finest cashmere. But a fine-tooth comb can catch pills while leaving the sweater intact. Lay the sweater on a flat surface, and run the comb flush against the garment, gently lifting the pills away.

SEWING ON A COAT BUTTON If it is sewed on too snugly, a button won't slide easily through its buttonhole, especially on thick fabrics such as wool. To ensure adequate give, place a matchstick between the button and the fabric, then sew around it to create a shank. Remove the matchstick, and twirl the end of the thread around the shank several times to reinforce it. Then pull the needle through the shank a few times to secure; snip the thread, and knot.

FIXING A PULLED HEM We used the cross-stitch (also called the catch stitch) to mend these cotton-Lycra pants, and red mercerized-cotton thread to illustrate (your thread and fabric should match).
1. Turn the pant leg inside out. Start and end your repair about ½ inch on either side of the rip. You don't have to knot your thread for mending; to secure it in the fabric, use a short backstitch: Piercing only the folded inner edge of the fabric, insert the needle in the hem, below the seam, and pull it out to make a ⅛-inch stitch. Reinsert the needle through the same stitch, and repeat once more to secure.
2. Just above the hem, on a slight diagonal from the backstitch, insert needle through fabric from right to left. Make the smallest possible stitch; it will show on the right side of the pants. Bring thread back down and to the right on a diagonal, and make a stitch in the hem, piercing only the top layer of fabric, again pushing the needle through from right to left. Inserting the needle from right to left will create tiny Xs.
3. Continue stitching up and down the hemline until the rip is closed. As you sew, keep the tension of the thread slightly loose; pulling it too tight could break it or pucker the fabric. Secure your work with a short backstitch, as at the start.

MENDING A RIPPED SEAM To mend the seam on this cotton shirt, we used mercerized-cotton thread (in red to illustrate; you should use thread that matches your fabric) and the even backstitch, one of the strongest hand stitches.
1. Turn the shirt inside out. Tie off the loose machine-stitched threads around the tear. To follow the original stitch line, draw a guideline with a marking pencil. To secure the thread, make a short backstitch about ½ inch before the rip, as described in "Fixing a Pulled Hem," above. This time, take the stitch through both layers of fabric. Insert the needle about ⅛ inch (half a stitch length) behind the point where the thread emerges, then pull the needle and thread out about ¼ inch (a full stitch length) forward. Continue stitching backward and forward until you've covered the area of the rip and stitched into the original seam for ½ inch. Finish again with a short backstitch. **2.** Now, depending on the garment's original seam finish, you can open the seam and press it flat, or finish the seam with an overcast stitch: From underneath, pull needle and thread through both pieces of fabric; then come up and over the seam allowance, on a slight diagonal, and reinsert needle and thread, being careful not to pull thread too taut. Repeat until repaired area is covered. Secure stitches with a short backstitch. Press seam.

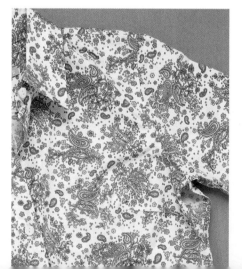
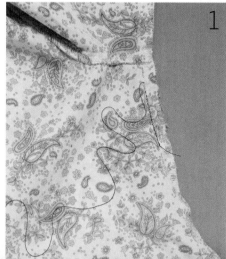
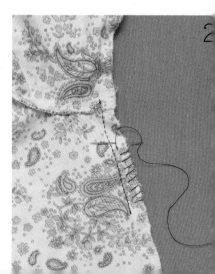

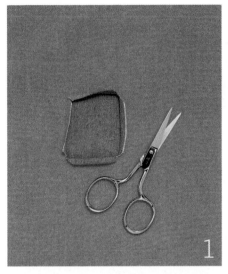

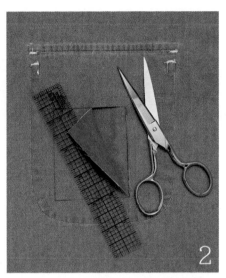

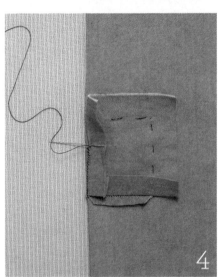

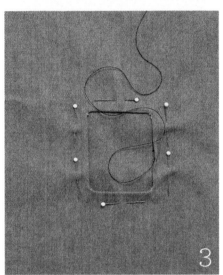

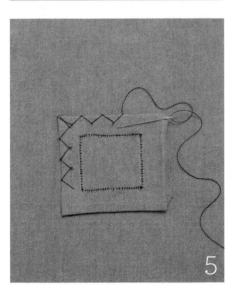

PATCHING A HOLE MATERIALS: *small and large pair of scissors ● fabric for the patch ● transparent ruler ● marking pencil ● pins ● needle and thread (some stitches will be visible, so thread color should match fabric)*

1. With small scissors, cut the hole into a clean square or rectangle. This will make the repair neater and easier. Trim any loose threads. At each corner of the square hole, cut a ¼-inch notch at a 45-degree angle. Turn material inside out, fold square's ¼-inch edges onto material's wrong side, and press them flat.

2. With the larger scissors, cut out the patch material; we cut ours from the back side of this shirt's pocket (the hole left behind can be patched later with another material, since it won't be visible). Measure, mark, and cut out a square that's ½ inch bigger all around than the hole you're repairing.

3. With the shirt still inside out, position patch on top of hole. If using a material with obvious grain, like denim, be sure to match up the patch and shirt so the grains run the same way. Turn material right side out, and pin patch in place. Now slip-baste the patch from the outside of the shirt: Starting anywhere on the square, make a ¼-inch stitch down through the patch; push the needle up and out, catching the folded edge of the hole. Continue all around the hole, and remove pins.

4. Turn the shirt inside out. Next, perform the overhand stitch, simply a tighter version of the overcast stitch described in "Mending a Ripped Seam," opposite: Fold back the ½-inch excess of patch fabric, so it's flush with the folded edge of the hole. Insert the needle down through the folded edge of the patch (only one layer of fabric), then stitch up diagonally through the folded edge of the shirt, joining the two fabrics. Continue this stitch in a uniform manner all around the square. Make several short backstitches at each corner to further secure the patch to the fabric. The overcast stitch will be slightly visible on the front of the shirt. Snip and pull out the basting thread.

5. To finish the edges of the patch inside the shirt, use the cross-stitch described in "Fixing A Pulled Hem," opposite. Cut off the tips of the four corners of the patch at 45-degree angles. Fold back each edge ¼ inch. Cross-stitch the edges to the shirt, picking up only one or two threads with each stitch. Press patch when finished.

VINEGAR LAUNDRY RINSE You can promote color-fastness in your new clothing and linens with this time-honored, easy treatment: Prerinse laundry in a solution of distilled white vinegar and cold water, using ⅔ cup vinegar for each gallon of water; let garments soak for up to fifteen minutes, then wash and dry according to the manufacturer's instructions.

STAIN-REMOVAL HOOP Stains on tablecloths or sheets are even harder to treat when you keep losing them among expanses of fabric. Frame the stain with an embroidery hoop to keep the area taut while you rinse the spot or apply stain removers. Isolating the spot also minimizes the chance that the stain will spread to other areas during treatment.

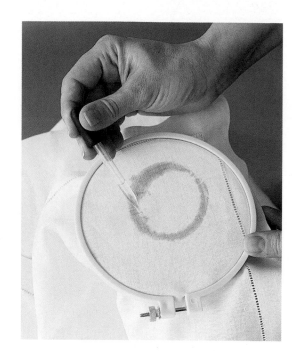

laundry tip Turning your clothes inside out every time you wash them will keep bright colors from fading, reduce pilling on outside surfaces, and minimize damage to snaps and buttons.

EVER-OPEN LAUNDRY BAG You'll be more apt to use a hanging laundry bag if you don't have to wrestle with the drawstring each time you want to deposit dirty clothes. Prop open the suspended bag with a large embroidery hoop, at least 14 inches in diameter, and you'll be able to drop in dirty clothes with ease. Plus, by hanging the bag up, you'll also save floor space.

HANDKERCHIEF SACHETS Keep your clothes smelling fresh with homemade sachets. Fill squares of inexpensive cotton with potpourri, cedar chips (a moth repellent), or a bar of scented soap. Tie each cloth into a pouch with string, and center it on a handkerchief (the cloth will protect the hanky from being stained by essential oils). Secure handkerchief around pouch with ribbon bows, and place sachets in closets and drawers.

HANGING STAIN CHART Knowing how to tackle a spot or spill is the first step toward removing it. To make a reference for treating the most stubborn stains, color-photocopy the chart on the opposite page, slide it into a clear plastic sleeve (available at office-supply stores), and place it in a clamp hanger. Suspend the hanger in your laundry area. Next time you find yourself facing a stained garment, just look up and follow the instructions. To keep even more cleaning information at your fingertips, copy the whitening chart on page 58 and hang it back-to-back with the stain guide.

FABRIC STAIN REMOVAL BASICS

This chart is for washable items only. The diluted dishwashing-soap solution called for below is made with 1 tablespoon of fragrance- and dye-free liquid soap (containing sodium laurel sulfate, or sodium laureth sulfate) and 9.5 ounces of water. Pour it into a tiny spray bottle. Do not use the enzyme detergent mentioned on protein fibers, such as silk, wool, cashmere, or angora. Always wash after using a dry solvent (such as mineral spirits or acetone), and do not use acetone on acetate.

stain	treatment
GREASE (butter, oil, mayonnaise)	Treat the area with a dry solvent (such as mineral spirits or acetone) in a well-ventilated room. Using an eyedropper, rinse with isopropyl alcohol; dry well. Spray the diluted dishwashing-soap solution on any remaining residue, and soak the item in an enzyme-detergent premix before washing.
PROTEIN (egg, blood)	Spray the diluted dishwashing-soap solution on the stain, and let it sit; rinse in tepid water. If the stain remains, treat the area with an enzyme detergent and wash according to label instructions.
FRUIT OR VEGETABLE (juice, jam)	Spray the diluted dishwashing-soap solution on the stain to remove the sugars. Using an eyedropper, flush the area with white vinegar and then hydrogen peroxide to remove any remaining color. Follow up with an enzyme detergent to remove residue before washing.
GRASS	Treat the area with a dry solvent in a well-ventilated room. Press with cheese-cloth; tamp with a soft-bristled brush. Repeat to remove as much pigment as possible. Flush area with isopropyl alcohol, tamp, and let dry. Follow up with an enzyme detergent to remove residue before washing.
RED WINE	Spray diluted dishwashing-soap solution on stain; tamp with a soft-bristled brush. Flush with water, apply white vinegar, and tamp; let stand several minutes, and flush again. If color remains, apply hydrogen peroxide and let stand. If color persists, apply 1 or 2 drops of ammonia to wet area. Flush with water. Treat with an enzyme detergent; wash. If color still remains, apply a powdered nonchlorinated color-safe bleach, such as sodium percarbonate; rewash.
WHITE WINE	Flush the stain with cold water, and spray with the diluted dishwashing-soap solution. Treat the area with an enzyme detergent, and then wash.
COFFEE OR TEA	Using an eyedropper, flush the area with lemon juice or white vinegar to remove color. Then treat with a stronger bleach, if necessary. To remove sugar or milk, spray area with the diluted dishwashing-soap solution, then wash with an enzyme detergent.
WAX OR GUM	Use ice to freeze wax or gum, or place item in the freezer; scrape or crack off as much as you can, then remove residue with an oil solvent or mineral spirits. Rinse with isopropyl alcohol; let dry. Treat with an enzyme detergent; wash.
LIPSTICK	Use a dull-edged knife to remove excess lipstick. Using an eyedropper, apply a dry solvent (such as mineral spirits or acetone) in a well-ventilated room; tamp with a soft-bristled brush. Flush the area with isopropyl alcohol, and tamp. Repeat until all color is removed, and let dry. Spray with diluted dishwashing-soap solution. Treat with an enzyme detergent, and wash.

stain	treatment
CHOCOLATE	Scrape off excess chocolate, and spray area with the diluted dishwashing-soap solution. Follow up with an enzyme detergent to remove residue before washing.
MUSTARD	Using an eyedropper, flush stain with vinegar; then wash with the diluted dishwashing-soap solution.
SAUCES (tomato, ketchup, barbecue)	Scrape off sauce; spray area with diluted dishwashing-soap solution. Soak in tepid water. If color remains, apply white vinegar with an eyedropper. Treat with an enzyme detergent; wash. If color persists, apply several drops of hydrogen peroxide; let sit. Rinse; treat again with enzyme detergent, and wash.
VINAIGRETTE	First, treat the stain as a grease stain (see treatment, top left). Then flush with white vinegar to remove any remaining color. Follow up with an enzyme detergent to remove residue before washing.
SOY SAUCE	Spray with diluted dishwashing-soap solution; tamp with a soft-bristled brush. Flush with water, apply white vinegar, and tamp; let stand several minutes, and flush again. If color remains, apply hydrogen peroxide and let stand. If color persists, apply 1 or 2 drops of ammonia to wet area. Flush with water. Treat with an enzyme detergent; wash. If color remains, apply a powdered nonchlorinated color-safe bleach, such as sodium percarbonate; rewash.
FELT-TIP INK	First, build a "dam" around the stain with mineral oil or petroleum jelly. Test the ink with a cotton swab saturated with water and another one saturated with isopropyl alcohol to determine whether the ink is oil-based or water-based. Whichever solvent pulls more pigment out of the stain is the one that should be used. If isopropyl alcohol is more effective, follow the steps for ballpoint ink stains below. If water is more effective, spray the stain with the diluted dishwashing-soap solution, and then flush with cold water. Always work within the confines of the dam.
MUD	If stain is a combination of mud and grass, treat grass stain first (see grass, left center). Shake or scrape off residue; pretreat stain with diluted dishwashing-soap solution, and soak. Then treat with an enzyme detergent; wash.
BALLPOINT INK	Build a "dam" around the stain with mineral oil or petroleum jelly. Treat area with isopropyl alcohol using an eyedropper. Remove any remaining pigment with a dry solvent in a well-ventilated room; let dry. Rinse with the diluted dishwashing-soap solution, then wash with an enzyme detergent in warm water. Always work within the confines of the dam.

WHITENING BASICS

Sometimes a gentle cleaning is all that's needed to restore a bright white. Try the mildest cleanser first (the first one in each category below). Always test a new product in a discreet spot.

material	cleanser	application
CANVAS (*tennis shoes, tote bags*)	Laundry detergent, powder or liquid Lemon juice	Sturdy canvas items can be machine laundered. For extra brightening, add lemon juice to the final rinse cycle, then let canvas dry in the sunlight.
CONCRETE (*garage floors, sidewalks*)	Powdered laundry detergent	Wet the concrete; then sprinkle detergent over stains, and scrub with a stiff-bristled brush. Rinse well. For oil stains, first soak up the oil with an absorbent, such as cat litter, then sweep away and wash.
CORIAN (*countertops and other hard synthetics*)	Abrasive cleanser Steel wool (without cleanser)	These synthetic surfaces are extremely durable and can stand up to scrubbing. Use an abrasive cleanser on a damp sponge, then rinse. For stubborn stains, scrub with fine-grade steel wool.
DELICATE FABRICS (*linens, lace*)	Mild laundry detergent Oxygen bleach Chlorine bleach (as last resort)	Hand-launder first with mild detergent. If fabric is still dingy, soak in a solution of ½ cup oxygen bleach and 2 gallons water. Treat tough stains on sturdier linens or lace with a weak chlorine-bleach solution: 1 teaspoon per gallon of water to start.
EARTHENWARE (*white ironstone, unpainted china*)	Hydrogen peroxide, commercial grade if available	In a covered plastic container, soak earthenware in hydrogen peroxide (do not dilute) for up to 3 days. Keep completely submerged and check often. Follow by soaking in distilled water. Never use chlorine bleach to clean earthenware.
GROUT (*tiled bathrooms*)	Baking soda Chlorine bleach	Wet grout first, then apply baking soda with a small scrub brush, working quickly in small areas so that the baking soda doesn't dissolve and lose abrasiveness. Rinse well. If necessary, spot-treat stubborn mildew with diluted chlorine bleach.
IVORY (*piano keys*)	Warm water Liquid dishwashing soap	Wipe each piano key with cheesecloth dampened with warm water. If necessary, use a drop of mild soap, then wipe again with a clean, damp cloth. Badly stained ivory should be buffed by a professional.
LAMINATES (*Formica countertops*)	Liquid dishwashing soap Baking soda Chlorine bleach	Follow manufacturer's instructions. Clean with a damp sponge and mild soap; rinse. Treat stains with a paste of baking soda and water, then rinse well. Use diluted chlorine bleach for tough stains; test first.
LEATHER AND SUEDE (*upholstery, shoes*)	Leather cleaner or saddle soap Lemon juice	Whiten leather upholstery with leather cleaner or saddle soap; let dry, and repeat, if necessary. For white suede, first remove surface dirt with a stiff-bristled brush; then rub with lemon juice, and leave item in the sunlight to dry.
PAINTED WALLS	Pine-oil cleanser Mild abrasive cleanser with bleach	Wipe down walls with a damp sponge periodically; for a more thorough cleaning, use pine-oil cleanser diluted in a bucket of water. If necessary, spot-treat stains with a dab of mild abrasive cleanser with bleach, and then rinse.
PORCELAIN (*sinks, bathtubs*)	Liquid dishwashing soap Baking soda Mild abrasive cleanser	Clean porcelain regularly with warm water and mild soap. For stains, use a mild abrasive, such as baking soda, or a mild abrasive cleanser on a damp sponge, and rinse well. Avoid harsh abrasives, which can scratch and dull the surface.
RUBBER AND HARD PLASTIC (*spatulas, cutting boards*)	Liquid dishwashing soap Chlorine bleach	Wash utensils in hot, soapy water after contact with any foods that may stain. Whiten and remove stubborn stains by soaking in a solution of equal parts chlorine bleach and water for an hour, checking periodically. Rinse well.
STONE (*floors, countertops*)	Liquid dishwashing soap White vinegar Marble cleanser	Follow manufacturer's instructions carefully, especially on polished marble surfaces, which can be damaged by anything harsher than warm water. For soap scum in stone showers, try a diluted mixture of vinegar and water; then rinse well.

BLEACHING LINENS

Chlorine bleach may be too potent for weekly use, but hand washing with it occasionally will keep sturdy linens looking their best. Experts recommend ¼ cup bleach per gallon of cool water, but start with a mixture half as strong. Soak for five minutes, then check progress. Use a wooden spoon to gently agitate. Be careful not to soak linens too long, and rinse them thoroughly.

WHITENING WITH BOILING WATER AND LEMON

Damask napkins, linens, even white socks can be brightened on the stove: Fill a pot with water and a few lemon slices, and bring to a boil. Turn off heat, add linens, and let soak for up to an hour; launder as usual. For extra whitening, spread them out in the sunlight to dry.

DOUBLE-DUTY CLEANSER

Erase coffee and tea stains from ceramic cups with denture-cleaning tablets. Fill the cup with warm water, and drop in a tablet. When the tablet is dissolved and the water is clear, empty the cup, and check the color. If the stain remains, repeat with new tablets, until all traces of the stain are gone. For whitening aged, dingy ceramics, see "Earthenware" on the whitening chart, opposite.

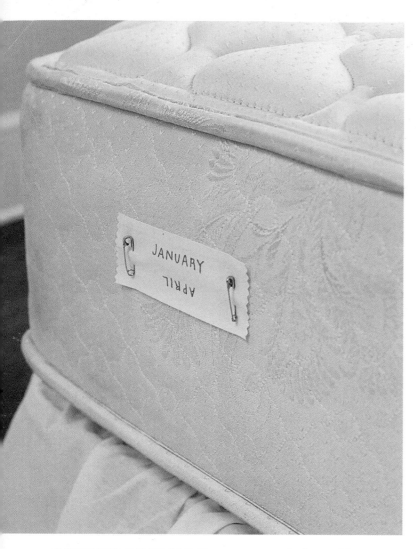

COORDINATING COMFORTER Instead of searching for a duvet cover to match your sheets or wall color, make your own using two flat sheets. Place them right sides together, then stitch around the perimeter with a ½-inch seam allowance, leaving an opening along the bottom that reaches to 24 inches from the corners (for queen-size sheets). Turn right side out. For fasteners, stitch twill-tape ties or Velcro tape along the two inside edges of the opening; or use buttons and buttonholes.

MATTRESS ROTATION For even wear and a longer life, a mattress should be flipped four times a year. Keep track by attaching two tags to the mattress with safety pins. Mark "January" (right side up) and "April" (upside down) on one end, and "October" (right side up) and "July" (upside down) on the other. When the appropriate month rolls around, turn and flip the mattress so that the appropriate month's name is right side up at the foot of the bed.

TO KEEP DOWN FLUFFY	
item	what to do
DOWN PILLOW	To prevent matting, throw pillow in the dryer with a clean, unused tennis ball or two.
DOWN JACKET	Place a clean, dry hand towel in the dryer with the jacket.
DOWN COMFORTER	Make sure comforter will fit in your dryer after it fluffs up; otherwise, bring to a professional.

BEDSIDE WATER GLASS Two ordinary glass tumblers combine to create a makeshift water carafe to keep on a bedside table. Simply fill a tall, narrow drinking glass, and cover it with a shorter, wider tumbler. Place the glasses on a small tray to catch drips and protect the table's surface; the bedside carafe will be especially appreciated by houseguests.

REVIVING CEDAR Cedar's fragrance (and its ability to repel moths) can fade over time. To maximize a chest (or other cedar piece's) ability to protect and perfume your woolens, simply rub the wood with fine-grit sandpaper whenever the odor starts to fade.

CHALK DEHUMIDIFIER A bundle of chalk hung in a closet will absorb excess moisture and keep clothing fresh and dry. Mount a hook in the closet, out of the way of clothes or linens, so the chalk won't brush against the fabric. Fasten a rubber band around a dozen pieces of chalk, and cover the band with seam binding or ribbon. Knot the seam binding, leaving a loop large enough for hanging the bundle.

SOAP SACHETS Some soaps are so intensely fragrant that they can be used as sachets to perfume clothes. Slip a bar or two of your favorite aromatic soap (with the paper wrapping left on) into a dresser drawer. Before the sweet smell fades, it will scent the drawer's contents for weeks and sometimes months.

book-freshening tip To remove the musty smell from an old book, wipe it clean with a barely damp soft cloth. Fill the bottom of a large garbage can with kitty litter. Place the book in a smaller can nested inside the large one, and cover the large can. Though this method isn't fool-proof, the book will usually be free of odor within a month.

LINEN DUST SHIELDS
To protect books from dust, hang crisp lengths of linen from book-shelves. The technique, tradition-ally used in Swedish libraries, also neatens the appearance of uneven volumes. Measure the length of the shelf, and the dis-tance from the shelf above to the top of the shortest book. Cut prewashed linen to this size plus 1 inch on all sides. Sew a 1-inch hem on bottom and sides, and stitch 1-inch-wide twill tape to the top edge. Fasten the shield to the underside of the shelf above with small nails or uphol-sterer's tacks every six inches.

ROTATING LAMPSHADES

Lampshades, especially those that sit near sunny spots, can fade unevenly over time. Keep them uniform in color by rotating them a half-turn each time you dust—about once a month is a good rule of thumb. This is especially important when you have a pair of matching lampshades. If one gets more sun than the other, move them between bases every other month.

PROPER BOOK CARE

Rather than tug a book off the shelf by the upper lip of its binding and risk damaging it, push in the books on each side of the volume you want, then pull it out by grasping both sides of its spine. To know where to return it, look for the two books that are pushed out of place.

HANGING DOORSTOP A good doorstop doesn't get underfoot when it's not in use—like this simple wedge, which hangs from a doorknob. Have a wooden wedge cut at a lumber store to measure 7 inches long, 3 inches wide, and 2 inches tall at its highest end. Drill a hole through the thick side using a ⅜- or ½-inch drill bit. Sand with fine-grain sandpaper. Stain or whitewash; don't use paint (it will chip). Cut grosgrain ribbon long enough to loop through the hole and over the knob, and tie.

CORD ANCHORS

Keep shades and blinds securely in place with drawer pulls, which make prettier anchors for cords than the usual hardware. We placed ½-inch-diameter pulls (available at hardware stores or home centers) 2½ inches apart alongside the window frame; then we wound the cords in a figure eight for a strong hold.

FINIAL DOORSTOP

Create an attractive doorstop using a ready-made drapery-rod or fence-post finial (available at home centers). Make sure its length is greater than the door-knob's. Paint or stain the ornament, then attach a rubber furniture bumper (below) to its top with a brad to prevent scratches and dents on the door. Screw the finial into the baseboard or wall a few inches above the floor, making sure it will make contact with the open door.

SECURING LIDS Top-shelf storage may protect your best china from kitchen bustle, but it can result in a crash when pieces are pulled from their lofty perch. Prevent lids from falling off by fastening the tops with a length of waxed twine. Wrap the twine securely around both vessel handles and over the lid, and then tie.

STACKING STORAGE China should be handled with care to avoid chips or scratches in the glaze. Paper plates, large baking cups, and felt rounds are just right for cradling dishes without adding bulk. Alternate dishes and inserts. Try paper coffee filters for bowls.

CHINA REPAIR There's an easy way to repair broken pieces of china. Partially fill a container such as a plastic storage bin with sand, then push the damaged vessel far enough into the sand so it won't wobble. Glue the handle in place, then let it dry completely sitting in the sand (leave overnight, if possible). Keep a bin filled halfway with sand in the garage to use for this purpose.

candle storage tip When not in use, keep candles in a dark, cool, dry place. Otherwise, light can fade the colors, heat can warp them, and excess moisture can make the wicks hard to ignite.

TAPER-CANDLE CARE

Loose candles can get jostled around and damaged easily in a drawer. Let paper-towel tubes come to the rescue—they're just the right shape and size for storing tapers. Wrap a pair of candles in a few layers of tissue paper, and slip the package into a cardboard tube. The tapers will be cushioned by the paper and cardboard. Label the cardboard with the candles' color and length so you can quickly find the ones you want.

STRING DISPENSER Bring a favorite flowerpot indoors, turn it upside down, and you have a charming way to keep your kitchen string neat and accessible. Choose a clean pot with a bright glaze, and place it over the ball of twine, threading the end through the drainage hole. Pull out the string and snip lengths for tying herb bouquets or trussing a chicken.

work surface tip

There is a secret hidden inside your kitchen drawer: extra counter space. Open the drawer, lay a large cutting board across its runners, then use your portable counter space to chop, stir, or hold ingredients while you cook.

SURFACE PROTECTOR Freezer paper, available at most grocery stores, can do more than just keep foods fresh. Roll out a sheet on a countertop or table the next time you are arranging flowers or working on a craft project using liquid that's apt to splash. Because the durable wrap has a plastic-coated side, it prevents moisture from seeping through and damaging wood surfaces.

EASY-GLIDE APPLIANCES
Countertop appliances such as coffeemakers and standing mixers are often stored pushed back under cupboards or shelves. But to use them, you need to pull them away from the wall. Self-adhesive felt pads—like those used to protect floors from furniture scratches—have another handy application. Stick them to the bottom of kitchen appliances to make them slide with ease without marring countertops.

REMOVING CARPET GHOSTS

To eliminate the indentations, or "ghosts," left by furniture in pile carpet, place ice cubes directly on the divots. The carpet fibers will swell as they absorb the water. Once the ghosts are gone, vacuum carpet thoroughly to pull up wet fibers.

SLIP-PROOFING RUGS

Keep natural-fiber area rugs in place and you'll help prevent slips and falls. To give a sisal or sea-grass area rug traction, flip it over, and apply lines of acrylic-latex caulk to the back every six inches or so. Once dry, the rubbery strips of caulk will hold it securely on the floor.

EASY FURNITURE MOVING

To avoid scuffed floors when rearranging heavy furniture—and to make the job easier—place a folded towel under each end before sliding the piece across the floor. Make sure the towels are clean, as dirty ones could scratch the floor.

NO-SLIP STAIRS

Make your steps nonskid with several stripes of homemade sand paint. Pick up a bag of sand at a craft or hardware store. Paint stairs with plain paint and let dry. Next, create a border for the stripes by outlining them with painter's tape. In a separate container, mix 2 cups paint with ¾ cup sand. Paint stripes with sand paint, keeping paint well stirred as you work. Let sand paint dry completely before removing the tape. Finish with another coat of the sand-free paint.

A SAFE STAIRCASE

Basement stairs are easier to see with fluorescent stripes added to the treads. You can use either fluorescent adhesive tape or paint; both are available at hardware stores. Begin with a clean, dust-free surface, then affix a strip of tape or apply a 1-inch stripe of paint 1 inch from the edge of each step. Putting the stripes back from the edge will minimize wear to the tape or paint and help keep it bright.

RUBBER-BAND DRIP
STOPPER Banish messy spills and drips when painting by sliding a rubber band over a paint can—perfect for small containers without handles. Each time you dip the paintbrush, wipe the bristles against the rubber band instead of the rim of the can. The rim will stay cleaner, making it easier to put the lid back on. You can also use this technique for varnish or polyurethane.

TIDY CORDS Eliminate the tangle of extension cords by storing each one in a piece of pipe-insulation, foam tubing with a slit along one side. Using a utility knife, cut the insulation to the desired length (about 13 inches for each 6 feet of cord). Measure then fold the cord, insert it into the tube, and label to indicate the length of the cord inside.

ROPE SAVER Banish frayed ends on a piece of rope: Lay one end of a piece of waxed twine against the rope, in the same direction as the strands. Secure twine by winding the remaining twine around rope, until at least ½-inch of the fraying portion is covered. Knot and cut twine.

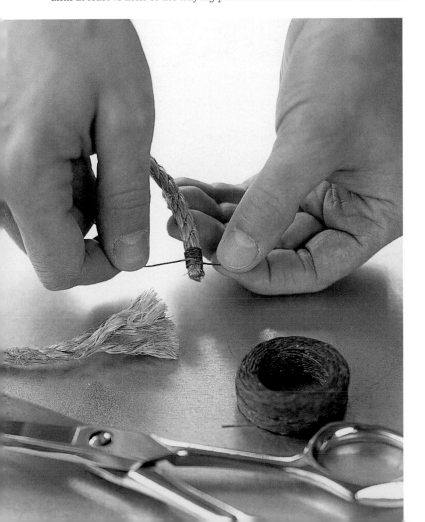

SMOOTHING CAULK
Unless you have experience using a caulk gun, the bead, or caulk width, can look inconsistent as it is applied. For a smoother, more attractive line, dip a plastic teaspoon into cool water and pull it along a newly caulked crevice. Dip the spoon in water periodically to keep it clean.

THAWING A LOCK

During the winter months, a frozen shed, house, or garage door can catch you off guard—and leave you out in the cold. Next time, try heating the key with a lighter, then carefully working the key in to thaw the lock. You may have to reheat the key a few times before it works. Keep a lighter in your car's glove compartment for just this purpose.

LOOSENING A LOCK

Locks can become stuck over time as debris builds up inside the keyhole. Before making an emergency trip to the hardware store for a spray lubricant, try rubbing a graphite pencil onto the edges of the key. Chances are the lock will open; graphite powder has a slick texture that reduces friction, allowing the key to slip in and turn more easily.

screw-loosening tip To loosen tightly set screws—even those stubbornly bonded to the wood with paint or varnish—place the tip of a screwdriver into the head of the screw and tap the handle of the driver with a hammer. The vibrations should knock the screw loose enough for easy extraction.

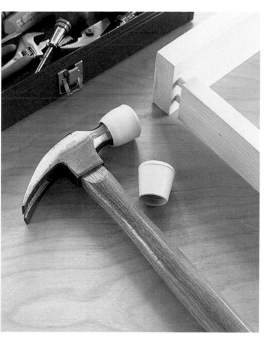

SHARPENING SCISSORS When scissors grow dull, it's tempting to replace them, or to pay an expert to sharpen them. But you can maintain the blades yourself, even without a sharpener. Fold extra-fine-grit sandpaper so that the grain faces out on both sides. Then simply make several clean cuts.

INSTANT MALLET
Convert an ordinary hammer into a rubber-headed mallet in seconds. For a standard-size hammer, slip a ¾- or 1-inch rubber tip, called a boot (they are usually used on furniture legs and are available at hardware stores), onto the hammer's head.

NEATER HOLES When hammering a nail into a wall, avoid marking or cracking the paint by covering the spot first with two pieces of adhesive tape, in a cross (above left). The tape will lift off without a trace. Be sure to hold the hammer near the bottom of its handle to minimize the number of strikes necessary. When pulling a nail out from a wall, (above center) prevent scuffing by putting a folded piece of cloth or paper towel beneath the hammer's head. Electric drills (above right) can shower plaster dust all over walls and floors. When drilling into a wall, hold a damp sponge beneath the drill to catch debris.

NAIL HOLDER Keep your fingers out of harm's way when driving a small finishing nail into a tight spot, such as the edge of a piece of molding. A small, rectangular magnet, available at hardware stores, can steady the nail for you. Use your free hand to hold the magnet up to the nail, and then hammer.

TOOL HEADLIGHT
When you're working in a dark corner, holding a flashlight and a tool at the same time can be difficult. Give a power drill its own spotlight. Secure a small flashlight to the side of the drill using two ¼-inch-wide rubber bands. Switch on the light, and you're ready to drill with precision.

WORK-SHELF LEDGE
To prevent items from falling off a shelf in your workspace, cut a 2-by-¼-inch piece of wood to the length of your shelf. Attach the trim with finishing nails, one about every foot. Set the nails with a punch; then, if desired, putty over the nail holes, sand, and paint.

There are many, many simple things that you can do to make your home more organized, more orderly, and smarter. This section introduces you to time- and space-saving tips that will definitely encourage you to get organized in all areas of your life, not just your closets and desktops and sewing rooms. –Martha

CLOSET DIVIDERS

To prevent stacks of clothing or linens from toppling or boxed items from shifting, divide your shelves into neat compartments with basic wooden shelf brackets, available at hardware stores. Look for brackets with long sides measuring just less than the height of your shelf and short sides equal to or just less than the depth. To install, place the shorter side of each bracket on the shelf and the longer side against the wall. Drill two wood screws into each bracket from the shelf's underside to secure.

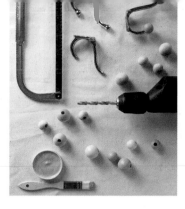

GENTLER COATRACK

MATERIALS: *wooden craft balls* ● *electric drill fitted with a wide bit* ● *hacksaw fitted with a metal-cutting blade* ● *latex or oil paint* ● *paintbrush*

The narrow ends of standard coat hooks can tug necklines out of shape and leave undesirable puckers in softer fabrics. Prevent such problems by replacing the hooks' tips with craft balls. Select balls large enough to accommodate the hooks (ours are ¾ and 1 inch in diameter). First, secure each ball in a vise, after wrapping it in a rag to prevent scratches. Drill about ½ inch deep. Next, secure hooks in the vise, cutting off ends using the hacksaw. Paint balls; let dry. Wedge the balls onto the ends of the hooks.

ORGANIZING LINENS

Keep whole sheet sets at the ready with this handy trick: Slip each set (a fitted sheet, a flat sheet, and one pillowcase) into the set's second pillowcase. The pillowcase, which serves as a storage sack, keeps the set together so you needn't search for matching pieces when you're making a bed. Store the sets by size.

WASHCLOTH MITT

For a generous source of lather and to put an end to searching for soap in the bathtub, slip a soap bar into a homemade mitt. Fold a washcloth in half with right side facing in, then cut it to the desired length. Tape a 2½-inch loop of cotton cord on the inside of the edge, about an inch from the uncut edge. Stitch along bottom and side edges, leaving a ¼-inch seam allowance, and catching the loop. Turn the pocket right side out; insert soap.

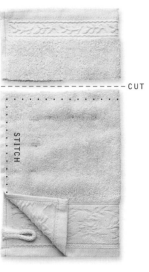

CUT

STITCH

soap solution

To use up remaining bits of bar soap, snip an opening in a natural sponge, and insert the pieces. Not only will this prevent messy soap residue from collecting in the soap dish, but the sponge, when wet, will yield a luxurious lather.

STACKED TOWEL BARS

Few bathrooms have enough places to hang towels. Stacking towel bars behind a closed door lets you remedy the shortage problem and use space efficiently. Three bars should fit comfortably. Moreover, a wooden door (as most are) provides a surface that is sturdier than wallboard or plaster. Hang the hardware according to manufacturer's instructions, spacing them down the length of the door.

POCKET TOWELS

Welcome houseguests with a few overnight essentials in these easy no-sew pocketed towels.

1. Lay out a standard hand towel, right side down, and fold up the bottom about a quarter of the way.

2. Turn the towel over, and fold in the long sides so that they overlap completely.

3. Flip the folded towel over again, and slide it over a larger towel hanging on the towel rack. Fill the pocket with toothpaste, a new toothbrush, and a washcloth—as well as a few extras such as bath salts and guest soaps.

1

2

3

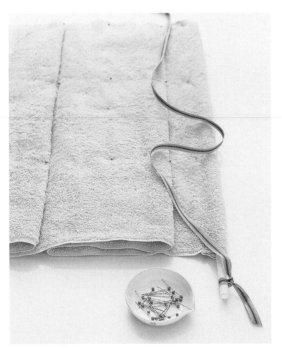

TERRY-CLOTH CADDY

Save space by storing toiletries in a hanging organizer: Fold down the top 1½ inches of a hand towel; pin, then sew to create a channel for a ½-inch diameter dowel (cut to 2-inches longer than the towel's width). Flip the towel and fold a pleat that overlaps about 5 inches; pin. Repeat to make a second pleat (far left), so bottom edge of towel is bottom edge of caddy; pin. Sew along both sides of the towel, leaving channel open; reinforce pocket's corners. Sew two more seams lengthwise to divide towel into thirds. Pass dowel through channel; tie a ribbon to both ends, and hang.

COORDINATED MISMATCHED TOWELS

Most linen closets hold a few perfectly usable towels that don't match. You can easily unify an assortment of solid-colored towels by trimming them with washable, decorative ribbon that complements each hue. Baste ribbon onto the right side of the towel along the dobby trim that is woven into most terry-cloth towels, or at a similar distance from the edge, usually 2 to 3 inches. Turn the ends of the ribbon under to create a neat edge. Machine stitch the ribbon in place using a small zigzag stitch.

MAGNETIC PIN HOLDER

This simple addition to your sewing kit will keep pins at hand—and in place. Add a magnet to a small ceramic dish and pins will stay put even if the dish tips. Using epoxy glue, affix a slim, wide, powerful magnet to the underside of a saucer or small dish.

MEASURING TABLE

This table makes clever use of unused space—namely, the edges—and eliminates the need to search for a yardstick. Purchase a metal measuring tape with peel-off adhesive from a home center, hardware store, or craft shop. Apply the tape to the perimeter of the work surface, uncovering the adhesive as you go, then snip off any excess tape with utility scissors.

MASON JAR SEWING KIT

With a few alterations, a jar with a two-part lid can be converted into a pincushion, and the container into a sewing kit. Separate the lid's sealer and screw cap. Trace the sealer's circumference onto cardboard; add 1 inch to that circle's diameter and, using a compass, draw the larger circle on a piece of linen or cotton fabric. Cut out both circles; stuff batting between fabric and cardboard. Turn the screw cap upside down; apply hot glue to the inside edge of the rim. Quickly press assembled cushion into lid until the cloth side protrudes in a smooth dome above screw cap and the cardboard is flush against the rim. Apply hot glue around the edge of the cardboard backing. Fold over excess fabric, and press to adhere. Glue the top of the sealer to the fabric-covered cardboard for a neat finish.

PINCUSHION WRAP

A pincushion that fastens onto your sewing machine is always within reach. Make a pattern: For length, measure the machine's circumference in a spot free of dials, then add 2½ inches. Choose a width that suits the machine (2 to 3 inches), and add ½ inch.

1. Layer a piece of thick fabric (for the backing) and a piece of cotton or velour (for the top) over two pieces of thin batting, all cut to fit dimensions.

2. Sew along three sides, leaving ¼-inch seam allowance.

3. Turn right side out, and top-stitch around all four sides, ¼ inch from edge. Sew strips of Velcro to ends on opposite sides.

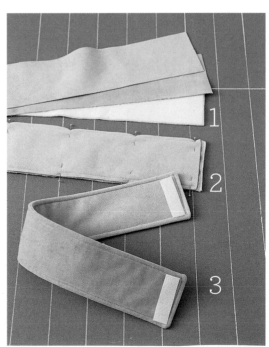

PAINT-CAN CUBBIES

Assign cans to be your storage spaces for bills, catalogs, and mail, or designate one for each member of the family. Line up a row of paint cans along a shelf, and cut Velcro strips that are slightly shorter than the length of each can. Peel the backing from one side of the Velcro, and apply it to the can; remove the backing from the other side, and affix it to a shelf in the desired spot. Center and adhere labels to the front edge of the shelf beneath the cans.

SANDPAPER ON FILE

With a simple system, you will never have to search through open packets or stray pieces of sandpaper trying to find (or guess which is) the right one. File sandpaper in an expandable folder by grit size and surface type. The next time you need a piece, you can just "look it up."

SAVING CRAFT REMNANTS Leftover project materials—odd lengths of ribbon and bits of paper—can get crumpled or lost. Keep them orderly with large clips hung on nails inside the door of a supply closet. Organize papers by size so you can see what you have; fold an index card over the paper layers to prevent dents from the clip. Suspend a pair of craft scissors from a string attached to one of the clips.

LEFTOVER PAINT STORAGE
Touch-up paint is essential to have on hand for dings and scratches on walls, but holding on to the original cans takes up too much space. Instead, transfer leftover paint from large cans to smaller vacuum-seal plastic tubs. Affix an adhesive label to the outside of the container, and note the room where the paint was used. Brush a color sample across the label for quick reference.

TACK-FREE BOARD

MATERIALS: *paint* ● *32-by-24-inch piece of plywood* ● *seven 24-inch lengths of ⅔-inch-wide screen molding* ● *wood glue* ● *nails*

Display favorite cards and photographs while protecting their surfaces from pinholes and tack marks (opposite). Paint plywood and molding strips in contrasting colors; let dry. Use glue and nails to fasten strips at distances ⅛ inch less than height of cards and photos you've chosen. To display, bow card or photo slightly, and tuck between strips.

WIRE-BASKET CATCHALL

Old-fashioned wire office baskets can help keep a small work table neat and ready for the next project, especially if the table lacks drawers. Mount a shallow basket to the wall, and use S-hooks to keep scissors and string suspended and off the work surface. Use cans suspended by O-rings in hooks to hold measuring tools and other accessories. Deeper wire baskets make coordinating containers for the tabletop.

ENVELOPE FOLDERS

Secure several envelopes together to hold letters, receipts, or business cards. Select the number of envelopes you want to join, then fold the flaps back on all but one. Stack them, open side up, with the unfolded envelope at the bottom. Moisten the adhesive on the folded flaps, and affix each to the envelope behind it. Punch a hole through the bottom center, place items in envelopes, and fold last flap over. Thread a decorative ribbon through the hole, wrap it around the stack, and tie.

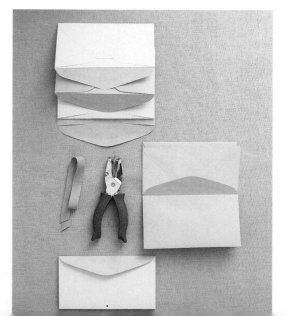

tape solution To save time and avoid frustration when trying to find the end of a roll of masking, duct, or packing tape, stick a bingo chip on the tape's loose end. For narrow tapes, such as translucent adhesive or double-stick tape, use a small button.

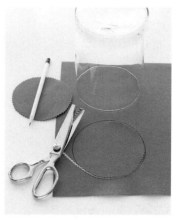

STRAIGHTENING SUPPLIES

Clear glass jars of various shapes and sizes make handy desktop containers for art and school supplies. To cushion the glass and protect scissor tips and pencil points, place a round of felt in the bottom of each jar. Trace the container's circumference onto felt; cut just inside the circle with pinking shears, since pinked edges allow the rounds to fit smoothly without buckling.

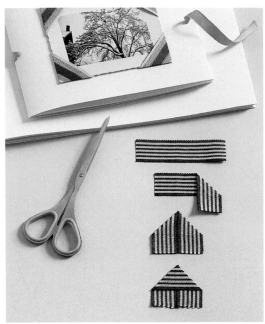

NO-GLUE SCRAPBOOK

When you return from vacation, it's time-consuming to try to organize all the receipts, ticket stubs, and maps you want to keep. Make it easy on yourself by filling a three-ring binder with plastic sleeves meant for business and baseball cards (opposite). Slide ticket stubs and postcards into compartments, or, if they don't fit, use a paper clip to attach them to a pocket. Trim maps, and slide them into the binder's outside sleeves (and spine) to make a decorative cover.

RIBBON PHOTO CORNERS

Recycle bits of pretty ribbon by using them to arrange favorite family photographs. Fold both ends of a 3-inch strip of grosgrain ribbon down at the midpoint to form a triangle; iron. Create two or four ribbons for each picture. Slip triangles—with seams in back—over corners of photos, and use acid-free double-sided photo tape to affix them to the album pages.

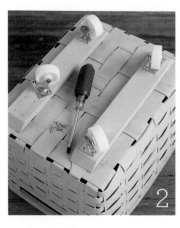

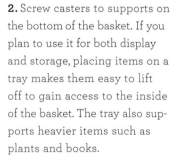

BASKET TABLE

MATERIALS: *sturdy lidded basket* ● *four 1-by-2s* ● *latex satin-finish paint* ● *paintbrush* ● *scrap lumber* ● *six 1¼-inch wood screws* ● *screwdriver* ● *4 casters with screws*

This mobile storage basket organizes clutter with the flip of the lid, and can be whisked off to wherever it's needed with ease.

1. Position two 1-by-2s, cut 2 inches shorter than the basket's length, inside basket 1 inch from each side. Align with second pair—cut the same length, ends mitered at a 45-degree angle and painted—placed on the underside with scrap lumber beneath for protection. From inside the basket, join the three layers with wood screws.

2. Screw casters to supports on the bottom of the basket. If you plan to use it for both display and storage, placing items on a tray makes them easy to lift off to gain access to the inside of the basket. The tray also supports heavier items such as plants and books.

SURPRISE DISPLAY MATERIALS: *ruler* ● *Homasote recycled-paper fiberboard* ● *pinking shears* ● *linen* ● *staple gun* ● *adhesive Velcro strips* ● Make the most of underused hutch or bookshelf space by installing a cloth-covered bulletin board inside. Wrapped in linen, the board is dressed up enough for any part of the house, and it makes a great surface for pinning up postcards, thank-you notes, favorite photos, and other mementos. Measure your space, and have a piece of Homasote cut ¼ inch smaller all around. Cut a piece of linen that's 2 inches larger all around. Lay the linen on a flat surface; center the board on top of the cloth. Pull the fabric over one side of the board and staple it in place. On the opposite side, pull the fabric taut, and staple. Repeat on the other two sides. Flip the board over; affix Velcro along the perimeter of the underside, about ⅛ inch from edge. Affix Velcro around the perimeter of the area to be covered on the bookshelf or hutch, measuring in ½ inch. Attach the board.

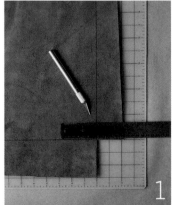

LEATHER TABLETOP MATERIALS: *table ● wood putty ● sandpaper ● straightedge ● leather (large enough to hang beyond bottom edge of tabletop on all sides) ● utility knife ● self-healing mat ● PVA adhesive ● upholstery tacks ●* Revitalize a scruffy side table (or coordinate mismatched tables) by adding a new leather surface. Putty or sand any holes or dents; the leather hides pits and scratches better than bumps and ridges. Measure tabletop and mark dimensions on the underside of leather. **1.** With a utility knife and straightedge, cut out a right-angled notch in each corner. Spread a thin layer of adhesive across tabletop. Lay out leather, right side up, and align notches with the corresponding corners. Smooth it out, pushing bubbles toward edges while keeping corners aligned. Once top is flat, spread glue on the four edges, and press leather into place. **2.** After glue has dried, trim excess leather. Finish with upholstery tacks.

LID-RACK MAIL SORTER

A wooden pot-lid rack is ideal
for holding mail; all it needs is a
fresh coat of paint. For easier
viewing, place smaller items, such
as letters, bills, and postcards,
near the front, and larger catalogs
and magazines toward the back.

HANDY MAGNET The most
convenient place for messages
may be the most convenient
place for keys, as well. Mount a
magnetic knife holder, available
at kitchen-supply stores, along
the bottom of a bulletin board
in your mudroom or entryway
to keep important items—keys,
scissors, even an emergency
flashlight—within reach. Secure
the magnetic strip with accom-
panying hardware to the frame
of the bulletin board.

cord ID solution

Leftover bread-bag clips make perfect identification tags for power cords. Write the name of a device on the unprinted side with a permanent marker, and slip it around the appropriate cord.

BATTERY-CHARGING DRAWER Keep your electronic devices running by creating a charging center. Choose a small table, such as a nightstand, with a back, a drawer, and an outlet close by. Drill aligning holes into the back of the table and the rear of the drawer. Affix adhesive wire clips to the drawer bottom and table back, near holes. Thread cords, leaving some of the line loose so the drawer can open; clip cords, and tie on a 5-ounce fishing weight behind the table (left) to take up the slack when the drawer is closed.

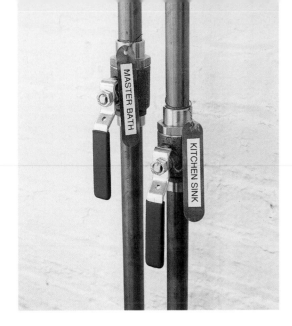

PIPE TAGS Dropping temperatures can cause pipes to freeze and burst. If you label the main shutoff valves ahead of time, you'll know exactly which ones to turn off to avert flooding. Print the name of the water source on a peel-off label (or use a personal label maker). Affix the labels to copper plant tags, and attach them to the corresponding pipes.

APPLIANCE MANUAL FOR GUESTS House-sitters, childcare providers, and guests may be baffled by the nuances of your stereo, DVD player, and climate-control and burglar-alarm systems. Provide them with a guide to using your keypads and remote controls. Type or write instructions and collect them in a convenient book or three-ring binder. Mark sections with tabs, one for each piece of equipment.

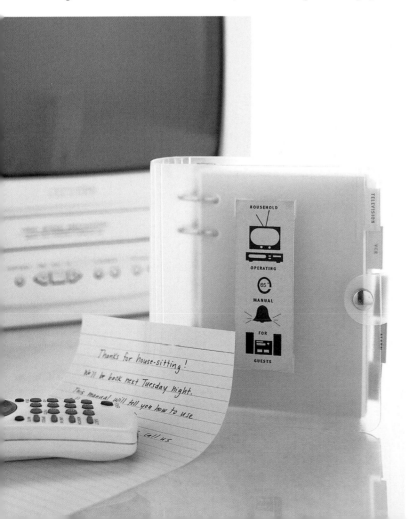

PIPE-AND-WIRE MAP
When the power goes out or the drain clogs is not the best time to figure out your house's interior workings. Sketch the floor plans, and indicate the shutoff valve, fuse, or power source for major items in your home that use water, gas, or electricity. Apply a color-coded sticker for each utility. Keep this map handy, and leave a copy for any house-sitter.

BAKING PAN "DRAWER"

Retrieving a jar of honey or bottle of oil from the back of a cupboard shelf can be awkward. For a simple fix, gather small items in a shallow baking pan, then treat it like a drawer, carefully sliding it in and out for easy access to everything. The pan will also catch drips, making cleanup easier.

PANTRY ORGANIZER

To keep serving trays, platters, and cutting boards accessible and orderly, divide them with tension rods, more commonly used to hang curtains. Measure the distance between two cupboard shelves, then position appropriate-size rods between them. Twist rods to tighten (inner springs will keep them upright). Use two rods on each side of the slots, spacing them according to the dimensions of the pieces you want to store inside.

pot-lid solution A pot rack hung from the ceiling saves space by keeping the vessels out of your way, but what about the lids? If they have looped handles, slip them over the pot's long handle. Then hang the entire unit on the rack.

CUPBOARD WINE RACK

Convert extra cabinet space into a wine repository (with wine glasses above and below). Use a space that is square, deep enough to hold bottles on their sides, and at least 14 inches tall and wide. Measure depth and diagonal distance between corners; cut two 1-by-12 boards to those dimensions, and sand to fit, if necessary. Notch middle of each piece at 90 degrees: Use a pencil and speed square to mark wood, and a jigsaw to make a ¾-inch-wide notch that stops at the center (below). Bisect pieces at notched points to make a three-dimensional X. Paint to match shelves.

PORTABLE CLEANING KIT

Make it easy to tote your cleaning supplies from one room to the next. Fill a plastic bucket with all-purpose and glass-cleaning sprays, a sponge, a toothbrush, a squeegee, a scrub brush, hopsack, and terry-cloth towels in washcloth and hand towel sizes. Between tasks, hang rubber gloves over the rim to dry.

ORDERLY UTILITY CLOSET

ORDERLY UTILITY CLOSET Standing mops and brooms upright in a corner of the utility closet can cause them to collect dirt and dust, as well as lose their shape. Instead, use tool hooks, available at hardware stores and home centers, to hang them on a wall or door with their "business ends" up. A dustpan, too, should be kept off the floor; hang it on a hook from the hole in its handle.

BUCKET HOSE STORAGE

Take better care of your garden hose by picking it up off the ground and draping it around a homemade caddy. Simply drill three holes in a triangular pattern into the bottom of a standard galvanized bucket. Depending on your wall surface, bolt or screw the bucket in place; use washers to strengthen the cut edges of the holes. A sprinkler will fit nicely inside the bucket, too.

FIREWOOD CARRIER

MATERIALS: *22-by-42-inch piece of canvas ● grommet kit ● hammer ● block of wood ● ½-inch grommets ● two 30-inch lengths of rope*

Create a convenient—and tidy—tool for carrying logs from the woodpile to the fireplace. Stitch a 1½-inch hem on each of the long sides of the canvas and a 2-inch hem on each of the short sides.

1. Using grommet kit, hammer, and wood block, drive two holes through the hem on each short side, 4½ inches from corners.

2. Secure grommets. Slip rope through grommets from finished side of canvas; knot the ends.

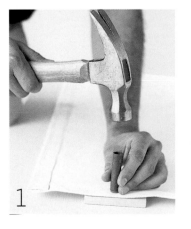

MOBILE RECYCLING BINS

Sorting your recyclables is one thing; getting them out to the curb is another. Wide stackable bins attached to a dolly can be wheeled outside, so you can unload your recyclables all at once and cut down on repeat trips. Screw metal label holders to the front of each bin with stove bolts (available at hardware stores); then attach the bottom bin to a wide dolly with utility drawer latches (also available at hardware stores).

UPRIGHT TOOL KIT MATERIALS: *metal or plastic bucket* ● *electric drill* ● *⅛-inch-thick plastic cable ties* ● Keep tools and supplies from sliding around in your utility bucket. Use a drill with a ⅛-inch bit to make an even number of holes around the bucket's rim, about 2 inches apart and 2 inches below the lip. Thread a plastic cable tie (available at hardware stores) through each pair of holes and secure outside the pail; inside, use small ties to fix each loop to the next for stability. Stand one tool in each loop, making sure its handle can be upright at full height, and store gloves or cloths in the pail's center.

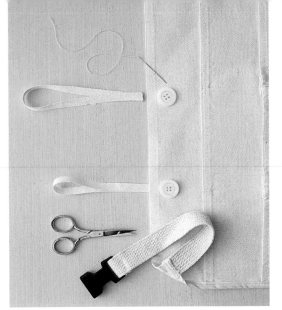

CUSTOMIZED TOTE POCKETS

Create convenient compartments for your tote. This three-pocket pouch is fashioned from a carpenter's canvas nail apron (available at hardware stores). Cut off the apron straps. Sew buttons and loops of twill tape (12-inch strips folded in half) to line up with tote's straps, 1 inch from top edge of the apron. Attach the button on top and the twill tape underneath. Place apron in tote; wrap twill tape around handles and pull buttons through hoops.

NO-SEW BASKET LINER

Dress up ordinary storage baskets—and make them easier to clean—with linings cut from oilcloth, a durable and moisture-resistant fabric that requires no hemming. Simply overlap two pieces crosswise in the basket, leaving several inches of overhang on each end before cutting. Hole-punch the oilcloth near the edges, and tie with ribbon to secure.

PERSONALIZED WELCOME MAT

MATERIALS: *18-by-30-inch coir doormat ● scissors ● masking tape in 3-inch and ¾-inch widths ● address numbers ● card stock ● utility knife ● ruler ● T-pins ● enamel spray paint in a contrasting color*

Make your address easy to identify by spray-painting the house numbers onto a coir doormat.

1. Create a border around the perimeter of the doormat with 3-inch tape; position it 1¼ inches from edges. For a second border, affix ¾-inch tape, leaving ½-inch between it and the 3-inch tape. Print out figures (ours are 650-point type), then photocopy each on card stock, and cut out with a utility knife; or choose 6-inch numbers from a hardware store. Use a ruler to center numbers; pin paper ones to mat.

2. Working in a well-ventilated area, hold can of paint 4 to 6 inches over mat and spray in small circles; bring can closer when spraying edges of mat.

3. Let dry at least 2 hours before removing tape and numbers.

DOORMAT BOOT SCRAPER

MATERIALS: *1-inch-thick marine-grade plywood* ● *coir doormat* ● *push-broom heads* ● *marine-grade varnish* ● *paintbrush* ● *drill* ● *wood screws*

Bring in flowers from the garden without tracking mud into the house. Have plywood cut to size at a home center: its width should be the same as the mat's; its length should equal the mat's plus the width of the broom heads. Apply marine-grade varnish to the plywood. With a drill, attach mat to plywood from above with wood screws; attach broom heads to board from below.

home-tool glossary You're more apt to tackle projects and repairs if your tools are comfortable, reliable, and simple to use, so purchase them with care. Store the tools in a plastic toolbox, which weighs less than a metal one and has the advantage of being rustproof. Since a small box may be outgrown quickly, choose one twice as large as you think you need; the extra space will also make tools easier to find.

TAPE MEASURE A sturdy, 1-inch-wide, 25-foot-long metal tape won't flop or waver. Look for a model with a blade-locking mechanism. Keep one in a utility drawer and another in the toolbox.

SCREWDRIVER Why is the screwdriver head you need always the one you don't have? Keep a driver such as this on hand, which holds single-slot and Phillips heads in its handle.

HAMMER A 16-ounce curved-claw hammer is the home-improvement equivalent of a chef's knife. It's a basic must-have, suitable for many household tasks. When hanging pictures, use a lighter hammer to prevent marring the surface of your wall.

LABEL MAKER This is an indispensable tool for organizing. Use it to label everything—jars, boxes, bins, shelves, drawers, files, photo albums—throughout the house.

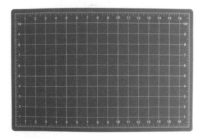

SELF-HEALING MAT The mat's soft upper layer melds back together after each cut, and two harder base layers keep blades from breaking through. A grid lets you measure as you work.

STAPLE GUN An all-purpose staple gun is perfect for decorating projects, such as stretching fabric or canvas on a frame, small upholstery jobs, or hanging tarps or holiday lights.

TRIANGLE Also called a speed square, this oft-overlooked implement lets you mark a perfect 90-degree angle. It's handy for do-it-yourself projects, such as building bookshelves.

UTILITY KNIFE This is essential for multiple tasks, including opening and breaking down cardboard boxes and making roof or trim repairs. For maximum efficiency and safety, change the blades regularly—dull blades are more dangerous than sharp ones.

GROMMET KIT With one of these, you can punch neat holes in any heavyweight fabric, such as canvas or vinyl, you wish to hang. The holes are then sealed with metal (usually brass) rings.

SANDPAPER Generally available in grades from 60 (coarsest) to 220 (finest), sandpaper is used to smooth or slightly roughen a surface. Paint will adhere better if you sand surfaces first.

CORDLESS DRILL For certain tasks, you can't do without a drill. A lightweight 9.6-volt drill with assorted bits is versatile and easy to use, even in tight spots. You can also purchase inserts to set square or hexagonal nuts.

CAULKING GUN Seal crevices with caulk to prevent drafts from windows or to protect bathroom and kitchen surfaces from water damage. A caulking gun can also apply adhesives.

HANDSAW Whether you're replacing molding, cutting boards, or taking on a small building project, this tool tends to get used often, primarily because it doesn't require electricity. The best handsaw for general use is one that is rugged and efficient but short enough to fit in a toolbox. Look for a handsaw with an open, comfortable handle and a sturdy blade. Keep and reuse the protective guard that comes with a new saw, even if it is made of cardboard.

PUTTY KNIFE This is used primarily to fill nail holes or dents in the wall. Keep the sharp edge free of nicks and scrapes, which will create unwanted patterns on anything you try to smooth.

TRELLIS ORGANIZER
Like vines, gardening tools can get entangled. A trellis makes a fitting ready-made grid from which to hang dozens of garden essentials. To attach the trellis to the wall of the shed or garage, drill a hole with a ⅛-inch bit at the top of every other vertical strip; then insert a 1¼-inch no.10 screw. Suspend tools from S-hooks; use paper clamps to hold items such as seed packs, which can't be hung from hooks.

GARDEN

Between the time you first scatter seeds over freshly turned soil and the time you pick the flowers that bloom, your garden will need steady maintenance. Even houseplants require ongoing care if they are to blossom and thrive. Indoor and outdoor gardeners alike rely on a combination of common sense and sophisticated science to make their gardens grow. Whether you would like to know how to water houseplants while you're on vacation, make your own rooting solution, or turn an ordinary bucket into a garden-tool caddy, you're bound to find something useful among the dozens of tips that follow. With that inspiration, you will have all the more reason to treat yourself to extra time in the garden.

Experienced gardeners are very inventive, and they know short-cuts and techniques that make seemingly complicated tasks a dream. But expert and novice gardeners alike can always use a helping hand; consider the ideas that follow just that. –Martha

PEDESTALS FOR PLANTS

Crowded together, potted plants can miss out on vital sunlight and ventilation, and remain hidden from view. Add rhythm and breathing space to your container-garden display, and allow trailing plants to hang free, by elevating some plants on "pedestals" of upended pots. Place low-growing plants in front and broad-leaved plants toward the rear, keeping their light and shade requirements in mind. Such pedestals can be as useful indoors as they are out.

**PURER HOUSEPLANT
WATER** Houseplants need a
healthy diet, too, and you can
help them by giving them water
you've purified yourself. Fill
jugs with water, and leave the
caps off for forty-eight hours.
The chlorine in the liquid will
evaporate, leaving cleaner
water behind. As a result, plants
will be able to get nutrients more
easily. It's important to feed
plants water that's at room temperature—more extreme temperatures can damage roots.

SOIL SAVER Most plants
don't need the entire depth of a
large container to thrive; some
annuals, for example, require
only 12 to 18 inches of soil. To
save soil and make the pot easier
to move, fill the bottom with
lightweight materials instead.
1. Place an upended plastic nursery
pot on the bottom; surround it
with polystyrene packing peanuts.
2. Cover with a layer of spun-
bonded polyester (available at
garden centers), then with soil.

Cushion the hard handles of spades, trowels, and rakes with plastic-foam pipe insulation. The tubes are slit end to end and can be cut to size, so you can easily slip them over any handle. Use duct tape to secure.

WIRE BASKET PLANT PROTECTOR Sometimes your pets are as attracted to the herb garden as you are. A wire filing basket, inverted and placed over small plants such as the catnip shown above, is a friendly way to keep little paws and curious noses at bay. The basket can be left in place for the entire growing season.

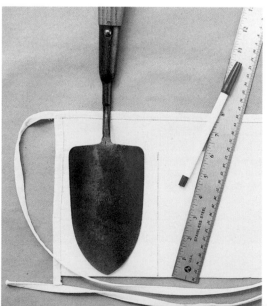

APRON TOOL HOLSTER
Create a miniature gardening center that you can tote while you tend your plants. Sew tool pockets into a carpenter's nail belt, which has one big pocket: Measure the width of each tool, such as a trowel, then add an inch for extra space. Use a pen to mark widths on the belt (left). Stitch along marks, creating pockets. Tie the belt around a bucket, which you can use to hold larger items or collect weeds.

GARDEN DEBRIS CARRIER

When gathering garden cuttings, weeds, or fallen twigs and branches, take along this lightweight tarp. You'll need 2 yards of 60-inch-wide cotton canvas and two closet poles or old broom handles about an inch thick and 62 inches long. Fold under the 60-inch ends of the canvas and machine-sew a 2-inch wide channel at each end. Slide the poles inside the channels to form handles. (If you don't have a sewing machine, you can use a staple gun to secure the cloth to the poles.) Spread the cloth and toss debris onto it. Pull the handles together and carry the folded cloth to the compost heap.

117
GARDEN TIPS

BAMBOO PLANT GUIDE

Use a handy garden reel, made from bamboo and heavy twine, to ensure straight rows when planting nursery stock. You will need two 1-foot-long pieces of ½- to ¾-inch bamboo for stakes. Cut one end of each stake at an angle to make it easier to push into the soil; with a file, notch the other end to keep the twine from slipping. Tie each end of a length of twine into the notch on the stake. The twine should be as long as your longest row; when laying out shorter rows, roll excess twine onto one of the stakes.

RESTORING GARDEN TOOLS

Like your hands, the handles of your favorite wood-handled garden tools suffer from overexposure to weather and soil. To renew splintered, dry, or cracked wood, sand the handles with medium-grit sandpaper; wipe clean. With a rag or disposable brush, coat the wood with a mix of equal parts linseed oil and turpentine. Let dry overnight; buff the handle with fine steel wool to remove any excess oil. For very worn wood, brush and buff a second time.

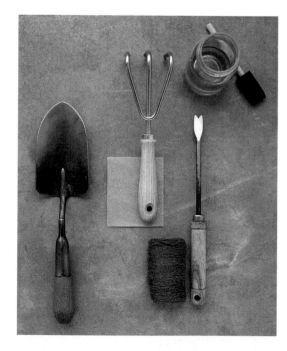

SEED-DEPTH INDICATOR

Using a gauge guarantees that seeds are sown at the right depth. To create your own marker, slide a rubber O-ring onto a dowel, positioning it at a measurement equal to the desired planting depth. Press the dowel into the soil, stopping at the O-ring. Plant seed in the hole.

SEED SHAKER Fine seeds, such as those of poppies, are difficult to sow evenly and almost as difficult to see. Sprinkle the seeds from a jar with a perforated lid—a grated-cheese jar, for instance—or make your own by puncturing a standard lid at even intervals with a small nail. Mix the seeds with sand that is a lighter color than the soil so you can see where you have sown.

EVENLY SPACED SEEDLINGS

Small plants should have enough space in the garden that they can flourish. To prevent crowding, transform the handle of a rake into a planting guide. Mark the handle with a permanent marker every six inches, then lay the rake down on top of the soil as you plant.

MINI GREENHOUSE Use an overturned jar to shelter a cutting from fluctuating temperatures and to maintain constant humidity. Take a 3- to 4-inch cutting from a nonflowering shoot that has at least three pairs of leaves, snipping just below a leaf node. Remove the lower leaves to expose two nodes. Dip the cutting into powdered rooting hormone. Using a pencil, make a hole in the soil. Insert the cutting to the depth of two nodes, firm the soil, and water. Place the jar over the cutting, and gently push it into the soil. Keep the cutting out of direct sunlight. Before doing this, check with a nursery or garden center to be sure your plant can be propagated this way.

seed-protection tip To prevent a small area of grass or wild-flower seed from washing away or being eaten by birds, cover the seeds with burlap or cheesecloth, staking it in place. Keep the soil wet during germination, gently watering through the burlap. Remove the covering as soon as you see the first sprouts.

OUTLINING A FLOWER BED

Defining the best contour for a new or expanded bed is easier when you plan ahead what it will look like. Use a rubber garden hose to lay out graceful curves. Shape and reshape the hose until you're satisfied with the design. Then fill a squeezable condiment bottle with powdered lime, and squirt it alongside the hose (below). Remove the hose before working with your spade.

PORTABLE LATH HOUSE

MATERIALS: *four 31-inch-long 1-by-2s* ● *twenty 36-inch-long 1-by-2s* ● *wood glue* ● *finishing nails* ● *2 galvanized butt hinges* ● *eight 1-inch screws* ● *latex paint (optional)*

This airy shelter can be moved wherever you need to shield tender seedlings or cuttings from full sun until they're well established. The 31-inch pieces will serve as the legs. Using the wood glue and finishing nails, attach the 36-inch strips to the legs, spacing them 1 inch apart along the entire length (below). (We used a 1-inch piece of wood as a spacer so we could align strips without having to measure.) Join the two lath panels with the butt hinges, attaching them to the undersides of legs with 1-inch screws. If desired, paint and let dry according to manufacturer's instructions.

tall grass tip
Ornamental grasses tend to flop over as a result of wind or rain. Surround the grass with a circle of bamboo stakes, then use twine to crisscross back and forth between the stakes to create a support web through which the grasses will grow.

INVASIVE BAMBOO Though the airy, open texture of bamboo is an attractive addition to many gardens, the plant has a notorious tendency to grow and spread. In fact, it's not unusual for bamboo to wander into neighboring beds up to 12 feet away. A terra-cotta chimney flue tile, submerged about a foot into the soil (with about 3 inches above the soil line) keeps the plant contained. Should any runners escape, shear them at the source, outside the flue.

INVISIBLE TRELLIS
Vines appear to defy gravity when they climb without supportive woodwork in sight. To help them thrive, create an inconspicuous network of wire and hooks on an exterior wall. Begin by making a grid: Install screw eyes 12 to 16 inches apart on the wall, then run medium-gauge wire through the hooks until the area is covered. For large expanses, place hooks every 2 feet. If the trellis will hold heavier climbers, such as roses, use heavy-gauge wire. Rust-resistant hooks and wire will prevent unsightly stains on siding.

TWINE DISPENSER

Carry twine to and from the garden without worrying it will roll away and unravel. Buy a clean paint can, slightly larger than your roll of string, at a home center or paint store. Make a hole in the center of the underside of the lid with a ¼-inch drill bit. Place the twine inside, and thread the end through the hole. Next time you need a piece, just tug and snip.

STORING FLOWERPOTS
Terra-cotta pots, stacked for storage, won't stick together or fall over if you use this handy rack. Drill ½-inch holes, spaced to accommodate the pots' diameters, into a 1-by-10 piece of wood. Apply wood glue to the bottom inch of ½-inch dowels (8 to 18 inches long), and insert them into the holes; dry overnight. Sandwich strips of corrugated cardboard between the pots.

GARDEN FILE
To create an indispensable garden reference, staple the top edges of your empty seed packets to index cards and file them in a recipe box. On the reverse, note when the seeds were sown, when they sprouted, or any other useful information for future seasons.

RAKE TOOL RACK An old metal rake head makes a creative—and useful—rack for hanging garden tools. Suspend trowels, weeders, hoes, or other small hand tools from the tines with lengths of cord. If your garden implements don't already have holes in the handles, create them using an electric drill fitted with a ³⁄₁₆-inch bit.

PLANT PLATFORM A weathered board and two large pots are all you need to make an attractive and functional garden shelf. Lay the board across the pots and use the surface as a staging area for plants on their way to the garden. Or showcase smaller specimens that might get overlooked on the ground. During the summer, the platform makes an ideal spot for setting out houseplants that would benefit from a little fresh air and sunshine.

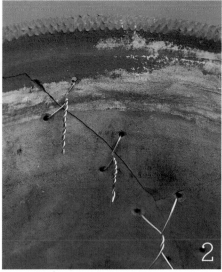

MENDING TERRA-COTTA POTS Frost and harsh weather conditions can cause condensation on a terra-cotta pot to freeze and expand, cracking the pot's porous surface. Suture a cracked pot to prevent it from breaking completely. **1.** Bind the empty pot around its circumference with lengths of twine at top and bottom. Using a ⅛-inch bit, drill a pair of holes, one on each side of the crack, 1 inch apart. Create additional pairs of holes as necessary, 3 to 4 inches from adjacent pairs of holes. **2.** Slip a 4-inch length of 20-gauge brass or copper wire through each pair of holes from the outside, twist wire tight, and smooth it flat against the inside of the pot. **3.** Remove twine and refill pot.

FUNGUS-FREE POTS

Terra-cotta is hospitable to plants, but fungus often sets up shop as well. Give your pots a good cleaning before stowing them for the winter and you'll help avoid such a problem. After removing plants, scrub and hose off any caked-on dirt, and soak pots overnight in a mixture of ½-cup bleach to every gallon of water. The next day, don a pair of rubber gloves (bleach may irritate your skin), and scrub the pots with a firm-bristled brush or nylon scouring pad. Rinse with clean water. Let pots dry thoroughly before storing.

WEATHERING PLASTIC

MATERIALS: *plastic garden pots ● acrylic paint in white, lime green, and moss green ● paintbrush ● sponge ● 60- or 70-grit sandpaper*

Embellished slightly with paint, faux-clay plastic pots are almost indistinguishable from those made of real terra-cotta.

1. Choose pots with lots of nooks and ridges, such as the basket-weave planter shown here.

2. Lightly brush white paint around the top of the pot, then paint around the bottom with moss green, making sure to leave a narrow space between the two. Dampen the sponge with water, and use it to apply the lime-green paint to the pot's midsection, overlapping the other colors.

3. Once the pot has dried, sand it, paying special attention to corners and edges.

AGING TERRA-COTTA

MATERIALS: *lime powder* ● *terra-cotta pots* ● *paintbrush* ● *plastic spray bottle* ● *150-grit sandpaper*

The whitened surface you sometimes see on a clay pot is the result of minerals that have leached from water over the years. Here's how to get that charming weathered look without waiting: Stir 1 cup lime powder, a mineral available at garden centers, into 2 cups water until it takes on a thick, gravylike consistency.

1. Brush the solution onto the pot, sparingly in some places, generously in others.

2. When the pot is completely coated and still wet, spray some areas with water (set the nozzle of your bottle on the "stream" setting), allowing some of the lime solution to run off.

3. Let the pot dry; sand the surface in a random pattern until you are satisfied with the mottled surface.

HOMEMADE ROOTING HORMONE Willow roots readily in water, releasing growth hormones called auxins that will stimulate the root growth of other plant cuttings. To make your own hormone solution, chop 3 or 4 willow twigs on an angle into 1- to 2-inch pieces and put into a large container. Cover with one gallon water, label the container, and leave for several days. Strain and reserve the water. Pour some into a jar the right size for the cuttings you want to root; pour the rest back into the original container. Let the cuttings stand overnight, then plant them in a rooting medium. Dilute the solution further, and use for watering the freshly planted cuttings.

WATERING WICK

Let your plants water themselves while you're on vacation. All it takes is an ingenious homemade wick. Cut a piece of nylon clothesline long enough to connect a water source to the plant; soak the rope for 30 minutes. Meanwhile, water and then drain the plant thoroughly. Bury one end of the wick deep in the soil and drop the other end in a container of water. (Use a water container that is taller or set higher than the potted plant.) For extra-large pots, use more than one wick.

plant-watering tip Even houseplants need a shower from time to time. Place the plants on a mat in the bathtub, and let a fine mist from the shower wash away dust from the leaves as it moistens the soil. If desired, blot leaves to prevent mineral spotting.

ROOTING IVY A "baby" plant attached to its nurturing parent will root faster. To propagate this way (a method called layering), extend a single stem from a parent plant and anchor it with a floral pin at the center of a 4-inch pot filled with potting mix. Keep both plants evenly moist and out of direct sunlight. In eight to ten weeks, the new growth can be cut away from the parent plant.

TENDER PLANTS
Tropical foliage plants, such as the coleus pictured above, are annuals in northern gardens. Winter-over hard-to-find varieties—and economize on houseplants—by taking cuttings from favorite tender plants. Trim lower leaves off the stems, and stand them in water-filled glasses until well rooted. Cuttings can then be potted and maintained indoors until spring.

ROTATING PLANTS

Always attracted to sunlight, potted plants living along a windowsill will become disproportionately leafy on one side. A quarter turn each day will prevent this. Simplify the task by placing the pots atop lazy Susans. Available in hardware and garden centers, the rotating platforms come in sizes that range from 3 to 18 inches in diameter. The larger sizes are useful for pots on the floor. Add surface protectors, such as the rubber bumpers pictured below, to the undersides of the lazy Susans.

POT SAUCER GUARDS

Protect furniture and floors by putting rubber bumpers under houseplants. Self-adhesive disks, intended for the backs of picture frames, are available at hardware stores. Three or four beneath each pot saucer will prevent scratching and keep moist terracotta from damaging wood.

HEALTHY PLANT TRAY Plants are most susceptible to insect infestation and other problems when the air is too dry. Create a humid environment to help them thrive: Fill the bottom of a watertight, rustproof metal tray (available at baking- and garden-supply stores) with pebbles. Arrange pots, and add water almost to the top of the pebbles. Water plants as usual.

HIDDEN LIGHT SOURCE

Fluorescent grow lights are good for houseplants, but not necessarily for décor. One clever solution is to conceal them behind the crown molding of a bookcase. Full-spectrum bulbs, available at home centers, promote the healthy growth and flowering of plants such as the myrtles and African violet shown here. Mount a fluorescent fixture to the underside of the top shelf with strips of self-adhesive Velcro, and drill a hole in the back of the bookcase for the electric cord.

AFRICAN VIOLET CARE

It's easy to keep an African violet looking attractive. Pinch off dead leaves, and when it develops a "neck" (an extra-long stem), remove the plant from the pot and cut some soil (an amount equal to the neck's length) from the base of the root ball (right). Repot with fresh soil, keeping the base leaves level with the rim. Dust leaves with a soft-bristled brush.

INDELIBLE PLANT LABELS

Most of us think that a pencil makes a less permanent mark than a pen does. But gardeners know that on a wooden or plastic plant label the opposite is true. In fact, you can even hide a penciled plastic label in the soil, submerging the writing, and it will remain legible indefinitely.

TRAVELING PLANTS

MATERIALS: *large, flat garden stone ● saw ● ¾-inch exterior plywood ● wood stain ● drill ● 4 casters with screws*

Heavy potted plants are easily moved with this homemade dolly. Begin by finding a flat stone that is large enough to hold the pot. Cut a piece of plywood into a square just smaller than the stone. Stain the plywood to match the stone's color; let dry. Drill holes, then secure casters to the plywood with screws. Set the stone on top of the plywood, then place the pot on the stone. Hold the pot when moving to avoid tipping.

REFRESHING TOPSOIL

Even a houseplant that doesn't
need repotting will benefit from
having its soil replenished once
a year. Remove 2 to 4 inches of
soil with a fork (its tines will
aerate the soil as you work), being
careful to avoid harming any
of the fragile feeder roots. Refill
the pot with fresh soil mixed
with slow-release fertilizer, and
if desired, top with gravel.

MINIATURE TOPIARY

Any vine or climbing houseplant
can be trained to grow into a
pleasing shape. Use needle-nose
pliers and medium-gauge wire
to create a coil or spiral form;
wrap the wire around a cylindrical
mold, such as a soup can, or a
conical shape, like a flowerpot.
Anchor a straight 4-inch length
in the soil of a young potted
plant. To prevent snags on the
other end, turn ½ inch of wire
back onto itself. Wind the vine
around the wire. Loosely tie new
growth to the form, if necessary.

PRUNING CONE-SHAPED SHRUBS A morning of pruning by eye can turn into an afternoon of trying to balance lopsided shrubs. With a tripod template as a guide, it's easier to trim plants into even, well-proportioned cones. Tie three bamboo poles of appropriate height together at the top. The bottoms of the poles can be spread out or pulled close together to form a broader or taller shape.

FULLER GERANIUMS

Geraniums will produce more leaves and flowers if you redistribute the plant's energy.

1. With pruning shears, cut off a section of the plant just above a leaf node and at least three nodes in length.

2. With a pencil, make a hole in the soil beside the plant, and slide in the cutting; pat the soil firm, and water. The cutting will take root without your having to add any extra hormones.

garden-tool glossary You need more than just your hands to plant and maintain a healthy garden; a selection of reliable tools makes tasks easier and improves results. Keep bladed tools sharp and their wooden handles oiled, especially when not in regular use. Although stainless steel won't rust, it needs to be cleaned. Hang tools up, rather than leaving them on the ground or propped against a wall.

SPRING RAKE While its primary use—gathering debris, such as fallen leaves, from lawns and garden beds—is apparent, a rake can also be used during the final grading of a fresh garden bed. Metal tines are more durable; bamboo ones are lighter and easier to wield.

HEDGE SHEARS In addition to maintaining hedges and topiaries, these are ideal for clipping grass around trees, walls, and fences. Hedge shears come in a variety of blade and handle lengths.

SHOVEL A long handle is best for heavy digging and lifting, such as when you break new ground. A shovel also comes in handy when transporting coarse mulch, leaf mold, or compost.

DANDELION SPIKE This is one of Martha's favorite garden tools. Use it whenever you need to do some light weeding or to aerate the soil around the root systems of your plants.

TROWEL Intended for planting small container plants, seedlings, and bulbs, a trowel is just right for weeding and cultivating. Keep one indoors for houseplants, and another in the potting shed.

HAND CULTIVATOR Designed to remove tenacious plants with deep tap-roots, such as dandelions, this tool's slim construction also allows you to weed cracks in paved or stone patios.

PRUNER Besides pruning, this is excellent for dead-heading, cutting flowers, snipping twine, cutting stakes, and pinching annuals. Try to purchase "bypass" shears, which cut with a clean, scissorslike action. Removable blades are easy to sharpen.

SPADE Cut and loosen soil first with a spade, then lift it with a shovel. Or use the spade to edge beds, cut and lift sod, or turn over a new garden bed. Buy one with metal straps that reinforce the handle.

ROSE AND WATERING WAND A wand allows easy watering of hanging baskets or any other plants that require an extended reach. The rose (at top, also called a water breaker) functions like a showerhead. Look for a model with multiple spray settings.

BEDDING RAKE Also known as a hard rake, this tool levels garden beds, moves soil, and removes large debris. It's also great for spreading mulch or compost over a bed that already exists.

LOPPERS This tool is useful when you want to remove branches that are too large to be cut with pruners. Loppers with long but lightweight aluminum handles provide leverage to slice through branches up to 2 inches thick. They are also more effective than a handsaw for cutting down small trees and more useful than a cultivator for clipping large weeds or coarse ornamental grasses.

Addresses and telephone numbers of sources may change prior to or following publication, as may availability of any item.

KITCHEN TIPS

● **PAGE 16** Cuisinart Mini-Prep PROCESSOR from Cuisinart, www.cuisinart.com for local retailers. Cedar serving TRAY from Dandelion, 888-548-1968 or www.tampopo.com.

● **PAGE 19** Garam masala SPICE MIX from Kalustyan's, 800-352-3451 or www.kalustyans.com.

● **PAGE 20** Martha Stewart Everyday Glass Refrigerator DISH WITH PLASTIC LID (#1367909), from Kmart; 800-866-0086 for store locations or www.kmart.com.

● **PAGE 22** "Rill" CASTERS from Ikea, 800-434-4532 or www.ikea.com.

● **PAGE 28** Waring bar BLENDER in stainless steel (KJU 005) or white (KJU 004), from Martha Stewart: The Catalog for Living; 800-950-7130 or www.marthastewart.com.

KITCHEN TECHNIQUES

● **PAGE 31** Great COARSE GRATER (KTZ 011), from Martha Stewart: The Catalog for Living; 800-950-7130 or www.marthastewart.com.

● **PAGE 35** Martha Stewart Everyday 3-Star 18/10 Stainless Steel STOCKPOT WITH LID, from Kmart; 800-866-0086 for store locations or www.kmart.com.

● **PAGE 36** Weber 18½" One-Touch Gold CHARCOAL GRILL, from Weber; 800-446-1071 or www.weber.com.

HOUSEHOLD HINTS

● **PAGE 49** GYM BASKETS (#427010), from the Container Store; 888-266-8246 or www.containerstore.com. LABELING KIT (OCR 008), from Martha Stewart: The Catalog for Living; 800-950-7130 or www.marthastewart.com. HARDWARE, from Gracious Home, 1220 Third Avenue, New York, NY 10021; 800-338-7809 or www.gracioushome.com.

● **PAGE 55** 14" wooden QUILTING HOOP, from The City Quilter, 133 West 25th Street, New York, NY 10001; 212-807-0390.

● **PAGE 56** Xyron 900 CRAFT MACHINE (CXR 005), from Martha Stewart: The Catalog for Living; 800-950-7130 or www.marthastewart.com.

● **PAGE 61** Martha Stewart Everyday 250-Thread Count Pima Cotton FLAT SHEET, from Kmart; 866-562-7848 or www.kmart.com.

● **PAGE 62** Charisma SHEETS by Fieldcrest (#7717 in truffle) and 90"-by-90"essential cotton BLANKET (#0537), in flax from Garnet Hill; 800-870-3513 or www.garnethill.com. Linen PULL SHADE, in Linen Ecru (#916), from Smith+Noble; 800-560-0027. Truncated resin CUBE LAMP by Darren Kearns, with black linen shade; for more information, call 212-533-1123.

● **PAGE 63** Chrome HOOK, from Restoration Hardware, 800-762-1005 or www.restoration-hardware.com.

● **PAGE 67** Kirsch DRAPERY HARD-WARE, also available in various sizes from BZI Inc., 318 Grand Street, New York, NY 10002; 212-966-6690.

● **PAGE 68** WAXED TWINE (CSC 003), from Martha Stewart: The Catalog for Living; 800-950-7130 or www.marthastewart.com.

● **PAGE 73** MARTHA STEWART EVERYDAY COLORS PAINT in Snapdragon (E12), available at Kmart; see above; also available from Sears; 800-972-4687 for locations. Benjamin Moore PORCH AND FLOOR ENAMEL PAINT, in haze gray (on porch), from Benjamin Moore; 800-672-4686 or www.benjaminmoore.com

ORGANIZING PROJECTS

● **PAGE 81** DOUBLE HOOK (#572MB26), and SINGLE HOOK (#581MB26), from Simon's Hardware & Bath, 421 Third Avenue, New York, NY 10016; 212-532-9220.

● **PAGE 85** WASHCLOTHS, HAND TOWELS, and BATH TOWELS, from Bed Bath & Beyond; 800-462-3966. RIBBON on towels, from M&J Trimmings, 1008 Sixth Avenue, New York, NY 10018; 212-391-6200.

● **PAGE 86** "Ingo" DINNER TABLE, from Ikea; 800-434-4532 or www.ikea.com. Starrett adhesive bench TAPE MEASURE (48"or 72" lengths), from Lee Valley Woodworking Tools Catalog; 800-871-8158. 1"-by-³⁄₁₆" disk MAGNET, from Forcefield, 2606 West Vine Drive, Fort Collins, CO 80521; 877-944-6247 or www.wondermagnet.com.

● **PAGE 88** 5-quart PAINT CAN (MPC160UL-P), from Basco, 800-776-3786 or www.bascousa.com/containers.

● **PAGE 89** Airtight CONTAINERS, from Martha Stewart Everyday, available at Kmart; 866-562-7848 or www.kmart.com. MAGAZINE HOLDER (DMH 001); and ORGANIZER BOX (OBS 001), from Martha Stewart: The Catalog for Living; 800-950-7130 or www.marthastewart.com.

● **PAGES 90-91** Select letterpress PRINTING SAMPLES, by Kerin Brooks Smith of Em Space Editions, 64 Van Steenbergh Lane, Shokan, NY 12481; 845-657-7203 or www.emspacestudios.com.

● **PAGE 93** PINKING SHEARS (CSG 002), and similar APOTHECARY JARS, from Martha Stewart: The Catalog for Living; 800-950-7130 or www.marthastewart.com.

● **PAGE 94** Assorted striped GROSGRAIN RIBBONS, from Mokuba New York, 55 West 39th Street, New York, NY 10018; 212-869-8900. Prati ALBUM in tan, 9¼" by 12", by special order from Kate's Paperie; 888-941-9169 or www.katespaperie.com.

● **PAGE 95** Avery Durable View ½" round LOCKING RING BINDER (#820928), in white, and Avery untabbed BUSINESS-CARD PAGES (#413371), from Staples, 800-378-2753 or www.staples.com. Similar SCRAPBOOK (CSN 004), from Martha Stewart: The Catalog for Living; 800-950-7130 or www.marthastewart.com.

● **PAGE 96** Large TASK BASKET with liner, in Natural (K325L/3), and MATCHING LID (K325C/3), from Basketville, 800-258-4553 for stores or www.basketville.com.

● **PAGE 98** LEATHER hides and remnants from Aadar Leather, 154 West 27th Street, New York, NY 10001; 212-647-9334. Jade PVA ADHESIVE from NY Central Art Supply, 62 Third Avenue, New York, NY 10003; 800-950-6111. Minimum order $15.

● **PAGE 99** "Grundtal" KNIFE MAGNET, from Ikea, 800-434-4532. Similar KNIFE MAGNETS, from Bed Bath & Beyond; 800-462-3966.

● **PAGE 100** "Smart" CHARGER from Thomas Distributing; 800-821-2769.

● **PAGE 101** TELEVISION, from Samsung.

● **PAGE 102** 11" to 16" TENSION BARS, from BZI, 212-966-6690. Great big MIXING BOWLS (KAB 002), from Martha Stewart: The Catalog for Living; 800-950-7130 or www.marthastewart.com.

● **PAGE 106** Stacking RECYCLING and STORAGE BINS, from The Container Store, 800-733-3532 or www.containerstore.com.

● **PAGE 107** Embroidery SCISSORS (CSG 003), from Martha Stewart: The Catalog for Living; 800-950-7130 or www.marthastewart.com. Rooster heavy-duty waist APRON (#53590), from Lowes, www.lowes.com.

● **PAGE 108** Plain coco DOORMAT, from Surprise! Surprise!, 91 Third Avenue, New York, NY 10003; 212-777-0990. MASKING TAPE and SPRAY PAINT, from New Hippodrome Hardware, 23 West 45th Street, New York, NY 10036; 212-840-2791.

GARDEN TIPS

● **PAGE 118** 4' BAMBOO POLES, from Bill's Flower Market; 816 Sixth Avenue, New York, NY 10001; 212 889 8154. HEMP TWINE, from Pearl Paint, 800-451-7327 or www.pearlpaint.com.

● **PAGE 121** POWDERED LIME, from The Home Depot; 800-430-3376.

● **PAGE 127** Basketweave TERRACOTTA POT, from Treillage, 418 East 75th Street, New York, NY 10021; 212-535-2288.

● **PAGE 129** Wedgwood CUP and SAUCER, part of a 5-piece place setting (KWW 001) from Martha Stewart: The Catalog for Living; 800-950-7130 or www.marthastewart.com.

● **PAGE 132** Cream FLOWERPOTS from Treillage; see above.

● **PAGE 133** Nineteenth-century BUTCHER'S TABLE, from Rooms & Gardens, 212-431-1297 or roomsandgardens.net. Black RIVER ROCKS from Chelsea Garden Center, 455 West 16th Street, New York, NY 10011; 212-929-2477.

● **PAGE 135** CASTERS from Garrett Wade, 800-221-2942 or www.garrettwade.com.

● **PAGE 137** Martha Stewart Everyday Garden BAMBOO STAKES, from Kmart; 800-866-0086 or www.kmart.com.

Executive Creative Director: ERIC A. PIKE

Editor: ELLEN MORRISSEY

Art Director: MARY JANE CALLISTER

Text by BETHANY LYTTLE

Associate Editor: CHRISTINE MOLLER

Design Assistant: JAMIE PROKELL

Copy Editor: ROBERT BOWE

Senior Design Production Associate: DUANE STAPP

Design Production Associate: MATTHEW LANDFIELD

Thank you to all who generously lent their time, talent, and energy to the creation of this book, among them Stephen Antonson, Annie Armstrong, Roger Astudillo, Evelyn Battaglia, Andrew Beckman, Tara Bench, Tony Bielaczyc, Rachel Boyle, Elizabeth Brownfield, Dora Braschi Cardinale, Denise Clappi, Peter Colen, Stephen Earle, Natalie Ermann, Richard P. Fontaine, Amanda Genge, Eric Hutton, Jennifer J. Jarett, Beth Krzyzkowski, Stacie McCormick, Jim McKeever, Kerri Mertaugh, Elizabeth Parson, Meg Peterson, George D. Planding, Lori Powell, Debra Puchalla, Meera Rao, Ben Rice, Margaret Roach, Colleen Shire, Lauren Podlach Stanich, Susan Sugarman, Timothy Tilghman, Gael Towey, Miranda Van Gelder, and Alison Vanek. Thanks also to Oxmoor House, Clarkson Potter, Satellite Graphics, AGT.seven, and R.R. Donnelley. Finally, many thanks to Martha, for teaching us that the most simple, straightforward ideas are always the most helpful.

PHOTOGRAPHERS

SANG AN pages 15 (bottom two), 23 (right), 24 (top right, bottom right), 28 (top right, bottom right), 43 (top right), 44 (top row), 54 (bottom), 55 (bottom two), 59, 60 (bottom), 63 (right), 86 (bottom), 87 (top), 89 (right), 107 (top two), 118 (bottom right), 132 (bottom right), 134

JIM BASTARDO page 99 (top two)

ANDREW BORDWIN pages 7 (left), 63 (top left), 90 (bottom two), 106 (top)

MONICA BUCK pages 12 (left), 31 (bottom left), 75 (bottom left), 102 (bottom), 104 (top), 137 (top)

EARL CARTER pages 16 (top), 40 (left)

SUSIE CUSHNER pages 31 (right), 136 (top left)

FORMULA Z/S pages 130 (bottom left), 132 (top two), 137 (bottom two)

SCOTT FRANCES page 4

DANA GALLAGHER pages 7 (right), 15 (top), 33, 34 (right), 35 (right), 41 (left), 71 (top), 85 (top two), 89 (left), 93, 95, 113, 118 (top left), 119, 124 (left), 127 (top row), 131 (left), 135 (bottom left)

GENTL & HYERS pages 11 (bottom left), 20 (center), 21, 42, 130 (top), 133

JOHN GRUEN pages 6, 14, 17, 19 (right), 20 (bottom right), 22 (bottom), 26 (left), 27 (right), 29, 35 (left), 36 (bottom), 38 (top), 54 (top), 65, 67 (bottom two), 74 (bottom), 79 (top), 81 (bottom), 82, 85 (bottom two), 86 (top two), 87 (bottom two), 106 (bottom two), 126, 131 (right)

LISA HUBBARD pages 1–3, 5 (top), 8, 20 (top right), 25 (bottom), 28 (left), 38 (bottom two), 39 (top row), 43 (top left, bottom left), 48, 49, 51 (bottom), 55 (top), 61, 63 (bottom left), 94, 102 (top), 103, 105, 107 (bottom two), 112, 114, 115

(top), 116, 117, 120 (top left), 121-123, 124 (top right), 125, 127 (bottom left), 128, 129

KARL JUENGEL pages 5 (middle and bottom), 46, 47, 74 (top left), 79 (middle), 110, 111, 138, 139

STEPHEN LEWIS pages 39 (bottom), 64, 66, 67 (top), 72 (top right, bottom right), 77 (left)

MAURA MCEVOY pages 11 (top), 25 (top), 36 (top two), 68 (left), 69, 71 (bottom two), 88 (top two), 92, 97, 120 (chart)

DAVID PRINCE pages 13 (right), 22 (top two), 23 (top), 24 (left), 26 (right), 27 (left), 32, 37, 51 (top), 52, 53, 56, 60 (top), 62, 68 (bottom right), 72 (left), 74 (top right), 75 (top left), 77 (right), 78 (bottom), 79 (bottom), 83, 88 (bottom), 90 (top), 91, 96, 101 (top left, center right), 104 (bottom right), 108, 109, 124 (bottom right), 136 (bottom right)

LISA ROMEREIN page 79 (bottom right)

CHARLES SCHILLER pages 10, 19 (bottom left), 50, 70, 75 (right), 80, 99 (bottom)

WENDELL T. WEBBER pages 9, 11 (right), 31 (top left), 34 (left), 40 (right), 45, 76 (top), 104 (left), 115 (bottom two), 135 (top right)

ANNA WILLIAMS pages 12 (right), 13 (left), 16 (left and bottom), 18, 30, 41 (right), 44 (bottom right), 68 (top), 73, 76 (bottom), 78 (top row), 81 (top two), 84, 98

JAY ZUKERKORN pages 23 (bottom left), 100, 101 (bottom left)

Front Cover:
LISA HUBBARD (all but the following)
PETER ARNELL (top right)
DAVID PRINCE (center right)
WENDELL T. WEBBER (bottom left, bottom center)

Back Cover: **DAVID PRINCE**